The Business of Therapy

The Business of Therapy
How to succeed in private practice

Pauline L Hodson
Illustrated by Clare Wood

Open University Press

Open University Press
McGraw-Hill Education
McGraw-Hill House
Shoppenhangers Road
Maidenhead
Berkshire
England
SL6 2QL

email: enquiries@openup.co.uk
world wide web: www.openup.co.uk

and Two Penn Plaza, New York, NY 10121-2289, USA

First published 2012

A catalogue record of this book is available from the British Library

ISBN-13: 978-0-33-524563-5 (pb)
ISBN-10: 0-33-524563-3 (pb)
eISBN: 978-0-33-524564-2

Library of Congress Cataloging-in-Publication Data
CIP data applied for

Typesetting and e-book compilations by
RefineCatch Limited, Bungay, Suffolk

Printed and bound by CPI Group (UK) Ltd, Croydon, CR0 4YY

"This book is a marvel! Packed with truly vital information both for the newly qualified and for the experienced therapist in private practice. The frequent vignettes and discussions are a delight, bringing a range of complex and challenging technical issues to life. This book gives an engaging and practical insight into what is usually the very private world of private practice"

Susanna Abse, CEO, The Tavistock Centre for Couple Relationships, London, UK

"I have often wondered just what goes on in therapy between psychotherapists and their clients in the secrecy of the consulting room. This book gives me an intriguing, bird's eye view from inside the room of how and why the process works."

Lisa Jayne Bloomer, Lisa Jayne Art Studio, UK

"Although addressed primarily to psychotherapists and counsellors, practically every page of this book applies equally to the practice of complementary medicine - acupuncture, osteopathy and so on - and it is essential reading for these practitioners. For it teaches, in far more depth than their training ever does, just what it means to be a therapist; and the book's clarity and wisdom will enhance the work done in any treatment room."

John Hamwee, Acupuncturist and author of Energy Medicine and Acupuncture for New Practitioners.

"A highly experienced and deeply wise practitioner of psychotherapy, Pauline Hodson serves as the most trustworthy of guides and mentors, providing mental health professionals with a cornucopia of illuminating advice about the crucial minutiae of our work. Written with admirable concision and with the page-turning delights of a fine novel, this book will be a joy for seasoned colleagues, and a life-saver for students and for those newly qualified. The Business of Therapy:

How to Succeed in Private Practice *leaves all other contenders in the dust!"*

Professor Brett Kahr, Centre for Child Mental Health in London and Roehampton University, UK

"I wish this marvellous book had come my way earlier. It's an essential read for any therapeutic practitioner, but particularly for those in their first years in the profession or who are still in training. Pauline Hodson has applied her extensive experience and 'know how' to create this valuable tool kit that covers all the practicalities, and much more, of running a private practice or clinic. Written with great heart but also in a boundaried psychodynamic style, The Business of Therapy *is practical, wise and down to earth without ever being prescriptive. It's a pleasure to recommend it."*

Carol Leader, Psychoanalytic Psychotherapist (BPC and UKCP)

For
Sarah and Rebecca

Contents

Acknowledgements		xiii
Foreword by Susie Orbach		xv
Preface		xvii
Introduction		1
1	**The Consulting Room**	3
	So what about your space?	5
	Access	5
	The bell	7
	Entrance hall	9
	The bathroom	10
	Quiet please, therapy in progress	10
	But is it clean?	11
	A breath of fresh air	12
	No one must know I am here	12
	First impressions	13
	The blank screen	14
	What about us?	16
	A shared room	16
	Clinics, institutions and the NHS	17
	Sometimes we have no choice	19
2	**The Clients**	21
	Getting started	22
	First impressions	23

Private practice   25
Finding clients   25
Professional registers   26
What do you do?   26
Developing your reputation   27
Raising your profile   29
The website   30
First encounters   31
Engaging with the client   32
Meeting   33
A fee-paying client   34

3   **Money Matters**   **37**
How do I know how much to charge?   39
What can the market bear?   40
Reviewing your fees   42
Billing   43
Payment   45
Unpaid bills   47
Holidays and missed sessions   48
Holidays   49
Missed sessions   51
Good practice   53

4   **Paperwork**   **54**
Stationery   54
Keep tidy   56
Referral systems   56
Professional letters   56
Professional notes   57
Confidentiality   59
Professional wills   59
Insurance   60
Income tax   61
Your home as your business   62

Continuing professional development (CPD)   64
Ethical issues   64
Data protection   66
Emails   67
The paper trail   67
A question of time   68

5   Boundaries   **70**
Protecting the client/therapist boundary   71
Neighbours   72
The boundary between you and your client   73
The boundary of time   76
The question of gifts and artefacts   78
Crossing the boundaries   79
Extending the therapeutic space   80
Telephone calls, emails and letters   81
Telephone sessions   82
The crisis telephone call   83
Couple work   84
The therapist's boundaries   85
The dependent therapist   85
Interest, curiosity or nosiness   86
Self-promotion   86
Invitations   87

6   Support Systems   **89**
A professional training   90
Theory   91
Therapy   91
Supervision   92
Recharging your batteries   93
Professional resources   94
A drink and a peer group   95
Inappropriate support   96
Family and friends   97

	When extra support is necessary	98
	Well-being	100
7	**Maintaining Your Practice**	**105**
	Feast or famine	106
	A movable feast	107
	Securing the business	108
	Taking a break	110
	Taking a sabbatical	112
	An unconscious choice	112
	Your professional community	113
	Mistakes	115
	Enactments	116
	But can we say 'No'?	118
	Trust your work and your colleagues	119
8	**Endings**	**120**
	Dilemmas	121
	Life is tough	121
	Interruptions	123
	A change of plan	125
	A fortunate profession	126
	A working retirement	127
	A critical mass	128
	Full retirement	129
	Planning ahead	129
	No gold clock	132
	A quiet affair	133
	Index	135

Acknowledgements

I would like to thank Candida Hunt and Sasha Brookes for their encouragement, friendship and professional help throughout the writing of this book. My thanks also to John Hamwee and Penny Jaques who were supportive of the idea from the outset, and to Rebecca Hodson who dashed off a list of 'things I would like to know about starting a therapeutic practice', within five minutes of my telling her of the project. I also want to thank Eirene Hardy who has maintained an interest in the development of the book; her thoughtful comments have been much appreciated. I am very grateful to the following friends and colleagues who have so generously contributed their thoughts and anecdotes. Sarah Hadland, Warren Colman, Marie Bradley, Lynn Baker, Evelyn Cleavley, Sohani Hayhurst, Jennifer Silverstone, David Zigmond, Helen Tarsh, Carol Leader, Oliver Howell and Ann Morton. I have drawn much material from my supervisees and of course my own caseload. Almost all I know about the business of therapy has been learned from my practice and I feel very fortunate indeed to have worked with so many interesting clients over the past 25 years. In order to respect the confidentiality of my clients and of clients of contributing therapists, most of the anecdotes which give substance and life to this book are a composite. I am grateful to Monika Lee, Senior Commissioning Editor at McGraw-Hill, for suggesting I write the book and for being most encouraging throughout, and to Clare Wood for her enthusiasm and for creating such excellent drawings, which reflect so well the tone of the book. Finally, I must thank Noel, my husband, for his help, encouragement and patience over the past 18 months. It would have been very difficult to write this book without his unflagging support.

The Green Door story in the Preface first appeared in *The Invisible Matrix: An Exploration of Professional Relationships in the Service of Psychotherapy*, edited by Sasha Brookes and Pauline L Hodson (Rebus Press, 2000) and is reproduced here with kind permission of the publisher.

Foreword

How do I charge? Should I have fresh flowers? Where do I want to set up my office? All such questions – and many more – are the exciting accompaniments to starting a practice. A therapist wants to put an individual stamp on the space she or he works from and the terms in which she or he offers therapy – but, like marriage, there is very little preparation or discussion. We absorb the consulting rooms where training, supervision and therapy have taken place, and they, like the parental relationship, form a template against and with which one creates one's own consulting space.

Questions of brightness, the comfort of the seating or lying, location – in or outside the home – how and where to greet patients, the arrangement of the loo, whether to share space or have one's own, can be ruminations of pleasure. And they should be. We are setting up a work home into which we invite people to explore the most private parts of themselves. Our accompanying them in their often difficult struggles, when words don't work and feelings overwhelm, requires not just our steadfastness but our thoughtfulness, reflectivity and compassion. We need to be alert and available. To beat where their heart beats, to hurt where they hurt and yet almost simultaneously to pull back so that we can think, analyse and illuminate what it hasn't been possible to see before.

To do this we need to be us. Not someone else. Not a cut-out of a therapist but the truest of who we are. We need to be as comfortable as we can so that we are alert to the other and yet know ourselves so well that when we are destabilized, when things are thrown at us, when the unexpected happens, our responses will have the veracity and complexity to meet the situation.

Setting up our spaces, the contract we make with the person, group or couple we are there for, becomes the expression of our containment. Our spaces are both practical and profound. They create the context so that the relationship can take whatever weight it needs to, as the troubles of those we see and offer therapy to layer onto its lap. As much as our patients, we need to be held. That holding will come from our confidence in knowing that we have created an environment that we are comfortable in, that we have colleagues we can connect and reflect with, that we are part of a larger community of psychotherapists. On all these points, Pauline Hodson guides us. She allows the seasoned therapist and the neophyte to think through what they want to provide and how they want to do it.

Most of what Pauline writes will enter into a reader's mind as smoothly as a perfect interpretation. It will simply make sense. Other things you will want to chew on – to enjoy the questions she raises and dispute even her suggestions in an open and embracing way.

This book, written with much love and affection, is a gift to our field. It should be handed out at every graduation or passing out ceremony. It should form the basis of Professional Practice seminars and sent to practitioners, beginners and those long in the tooth, who will feel invigorated by its suggestions.

Susie Orbach
London, March 2012

Preface

We spend much time caught up in the microcosm of our clients' lives and this book encourages an attention to detail that will help to ensure a safe space within which our work can take place. Of course it is not always the case that therapy reaches a satisfactory conclusion. I can feel despondent and wonder about the value of my work when a couple leave therapy having been unable to resolve their difficulties; or an individual client decides therapy is not for him. But more often than not, as I say goodbye to a client for the last time, I feel the satisfaction that significant changes have taken place in the containing space of my consulting room.

The following story, 'The Green Door' (Hodson & Brookes, 2000) paints a wider view and in so doing reminds us of the value of our work and why we do it. It illustrates so clearly what the business of therapy is all about. It shows how rewarding it is for both client and therapist when transformative work takes place over a period of time and life changes for the better. It demonstrates why we are in *The Business of Therapy*.

The Green Door

It is five minutes to four o'clock and the new client is due to arrive at four. The therapist checks to make sure all is ready. The diary tells her the name of this new client and who referred him, and she remembers the brief telephone call in which he told her that he had a relationship problem, but his wife would not consider therapy. He told the therapist that he worked at home so could manage an appointment during the day. He sounded brisk and cheerful but his manner belied the message. His wife was about to leave him.

It is five minutes to four o'clock and the client looks anxiously at his watch. Perhaps he should wait a little longer, he does not want to be early: don't therapists have a thing about time? He looks at the house, noticing the geraniums on the step and the green front door. The house looks welcoming but he feels a knot in his stomach. She had sounded efficient and gentle on the telephone but had asked him few questions. The tenor of her voice told him little about her age; was she middle aged like him; married or single; did she have children; would she have any idea of the difficulties he was going through with his wife and children? Was he doing the right thing in approaching a therapist at all?

It is four o'clock and the door bell rings, there is a pause, therapist and client on opposite sides of the green front door gather themselves for their first meeting, maybe the first of very many meetings. They are about to enter what Joyce McDougall has called the theatre of the mind.[1] The stage has been set; the consulting room will remain the same for as long as their relationship continues and it seems as if there are just two people who will occupy it.

But both client and therapist carry within them invisible matrices. The client's unconscious matrix of relationships, both past and present, will slowly over time be explored and will become visible to both of the people on the therapeutic stage; but what of the therapist's personal and professional matrices? They will remain invisible to the client, but the therapist's professional matrix, which is such a crucial aspect of the therapeutic container, will play as important a part as any other in the client's matrix of relationships, in the drama that is about to take place.

It is ten to five and the client, after very many sessions, leaves for the last time by the green front door. There are winter pansies in the

1 McDougall, J (1986) *Theatres of the Mind.* New York: Basic Books.

pot where the geraniums were that summer four and a half years ago. He walks down the steps and turns towards his car. He no longer has an anxious knot in his stomach, but feels a sense of sadness mixed with elation. He will miss his therapist.

It is ten to five and the therapist watches for the last time the back of her client as he closes the green front door. She feels a mixture of feelings, including a sense of loss, but also a real pleasure that after many sessions her client has discovered much about himself and his relationships. He can now make decisions and choices based on an intimate knowledge of who he is and he is enjoying, perhaps for the first time, his family life.

It is five o'clock and the client negotiates his way through the traffic, he is alone but he does not feel lonely, through his therapy he has discovered a rich internal matrix of relationships which nourish and sustain him. Therapy was the right decision after all; he feels a sense of gratitude towards his therapist.

It is five o'clock; the therapist opens the client's file and reads once again the referrer's notes. As she writes the final report she thinks of her supervisor and reflects on the hours of supervision she has had on this client. Her supervisor knows him almost as well as she does. Glancing through her notes she remembers with a smile the complexity of negotiating her way through his decision to see a marital therapist with his wife. That was two years ago. The combination of therapies had worked well, but there had been some sticky moments.

By six o'clock the therapeutic stage is empty, the two players have left and the drama that has been such an important part of the client's life and that has occupied a great deal of time in the therapist's professional life is over. Different aspects of the client's internal world of unconscious relationships have taken centre stage from time to time, made conscious through the relationship with his therapist, who has remained a willing consort available for different roles ascribed to her. Her capacity to take part in the drama, while observing and interpreting it, has been strengthened by a professional matrix, a supporting cast which now waits backstage for the next play to begin.

Pauline L Hodson
Oxford, February 2012

Introduction

To be trained as a psychotherapist or counsellor is an exciting and rewarding experience.

I enjoyed my training enormously and found the focus, which was almost exclusively on my theoretical, clinical and psychological development, to be of great value both personally and professionally. I emerged confident in the quality of the training I had received, but quite quickly realized how much else there was to think about if I was to provide my clients with the safe working environment they needed for good and sensitive work to take place. I had internalized the integrity of my training institution, which has stood me in good stead throughout my working life, but the matter of setting up in private practice had not been directly addressed. I did not know where to turn for the guidance I needed.

Now, many years later, it has been a great pleasure to write this book that is – more or less – the one I wished was available as I was embarking on my career.

The intention of this book is to bridge the gap between the clinical work carried out under the auspices of a training body and its application to the wider world. I hope it will be both a resource for students who are completing, or have finished, their training and are considering private practice, and also of value to the experienced therapist.

From creating a comfortable consulting room to grappling with the thorny question of money, from finding clients to accessing insurance cover, the first four chapters of the book tackle both the psychological and practical issues which need to be addressed before we open our doors for business.

The following three chapters address issues that arise once a therapy practice is established, including boundaries, support systems and maintaining your practice. It is important to be able to anticipate and think about situations that impinge on the work, such as illness, holidays, building works, pets and children – the vicissitudes of life which have no respect for the sanctity of the consulting room, but which if not paid attention to can disrupt the safe working environment.

The final chapter deals with endings: with clients when they come to the end of their therapy and for therapists as they come towards the end of their working lives.

Whatever the therapist's situation, it is her primary duty to provide the client with a safe, secure and protected space in which to work. This requires constant vigilance by the therapist of both her internal and external worlds. If we are ill prepared and anxious we will not be able to contain our clients.

Rather like the Russian dolls where one is contained inside the other, if the therapist feels contained by her environment she will be able to contain her client; if the client feels contained he will feel safe enough to trust himself to the process. Containment is a fundamental principle of psychoanalytic work and I believe it underpins therapeutic work of whatever kind.

I have used anecdote as a way of illustrating the wide variety of issues that most working therapists will encounter during the course of a career. Respected colleagues have contributed their experiences, and I have used my own case work for the anecdotes, but in all cases clients' confidentiality is protected.

For the sake of clarity and understanding, I have given all the therapists a female identity and all the clients a male one. As a rule the practitioner is identified as 'a therapist' and a customer as 'a client', but when necessary and appropriate the practitioner is defined as a counsellor, psychotherapist or psychoanalyst. In some circumstances the client is referred to as a patient.

I hope, whether you are just starting out or have been in practice for some time, that you find this book useful and enjoyable.

1

The Consulting Room

A colleague of mine always left a light on in her consulting room
window, which faced onto the road. She did this because once,
when she had been in therapy herself and feeling quite desperate,
she had driven round to her therapist's house at night and been
comforted to see a light in her therapist's window.

This anecdote illustrates how much our clients invest in our
working space and how important it can be to them; the space
is important to us too. Rather like the Russian dolls where one
doll is contained by another we could say that our consulting
room is the outer doll, the outer container. Our work space, our
consulting room, needs to be paid attention to before any work
can be done.

Our environment is important because in order for us to
do good work we need to feel that we have a safe, reliable and
predictable place in which to do it. There will often be times
when personal difficulties threaten to impinge on our professional
lives and it is at such times that we will particularly appreciate
the effort we have put into the making of our rooms. Just as our
clients do, when we enter our consulting room we will enter a
space that is both timeless and predictable – a container for both
us and our clients.

There are huge differences in private consulting rooms, which
can range from gloomy basements to airy garrets; some of us will
have waiting rooms, but often there is not enough space for one.
I know of one therapist who saw her clients, very successfully,

in a small hut at the side of her canal boat. For practitioners who decide to rent rooms in a clinic or share rooms it can be challenging to make the place feel like their own.

> How could I engage with him as a therapist? There was a dead plant in the hall – if he can't even keep a plant alive how could he possibly help me?

From dead flowers in the hall to overflowing waste paper baskets there are many ways a practitioner can unwittingly show disregard for her clients. Rarely do our clients remark on the ways in which we conduct our business, but that does not mean that they do not notice, form opinions or judge us on our working environment. Just as we observe and draw conclusions about our potential clients in the initial consultation, so do they of us.

So how we set up our rooms is important from both a practical and a psychological point of view. By paying close attention to the practical needs of the client and anticipating possible problems we can, whatever our circumstances, create a safe and containing space which is crucial if good work is to be done.

> My consulting room is on the third floor of my house. Ours is a very busy household and often quite noisy. There is a lot to contend with: neighbours, children, dogs, cats and a husband who works at home. The choice of the room on the top floor has its advantages and disadvantages. It is good because I am far away from the general hustle and bustle of domestic life, but it is very, very small, just room enough for a desk under the window, two chairs for my clients and one for me.

It has an extra door which ensures privacy and quietness and helps me to relax as I know we cannot be overheard. It must be reassuring for my clients too who, of course, notice both doors when they enter the room. Chairs were a problem, as by necessity they have to be small but I found some basketwork ones which are upright and have arms. They fit into the room, look good and are surprisingly comfortable.

The room has a large window which looks out over tree tops, and I have positioned the chairs so that my clients have the view and a sense of space. I really like my consulting room, it is warm and often sunny, it is quiet and the view is lovely. It is a containing space and when I am up here in my eyrie I feel removed from my domestic life and able to concentrate on my work without worrying about life downstairs.

So what about your space?

First, you will need to decide whether to use your home or to rent a room elsewhere. There are consequences attached to both options and your decision will depend very much on your circumstances. Obviously if there is absolutely no extra space that could be used as a consulting room in your house the decision is made for you, but take a good look and think imaginatively; consider our therapist on the canal boat – I heard that clients loved the tiny hut that she used as her consulting room.

Access

You will have given the client directions over the telephone, you might even have a printed map to post or email to them. It is helpful to tell clients where they can park if they are coming by car, and of course where the trains, bus stops and tube stations are if they are using public transport. If you are not sending a map, do be really clear about directions; if your client is anxious or upset or both he might not take in all your instructions. It will help him greatly to hear that you have been thoughtful enough to anticipate any problems he might have in finding you or parking.

You will need to consider disabled access. You might find that if you use a little ingenuity you can accommodate a wheelchair, but if that is impossible you can be clear to anyone who asks that this is the case. Some clients may need to know if the access to your consulting room is particularly difficult, as there will be people who will find stairs hard to negotiate.

When it is not clear where the consulting room is in relation to the property you might arrange to meet your client at the front gate and lead them to the consulting room. For instance, if the consulting room is in a separate building from your house it is helpful to let clients know, so that when you meet them they are already prepared and are not expecting to be taken into the main house. Such attention to detail can make a big difference to the clients' first impression of you; instead of their minds being full of anxious questions such as, Where am I going? Why isn't she letting me into the house? Am I safe? they will be able to trust that you are thoughtful and have their best interests at heart.

Any misunderstanding or confusion about arrangements during the negotiations surrounding those first consultations can result in losing the client.

Twenty-five years on I still remember with regret how I lost my very first clients who misunderstood my directions. I live opposite a green, but my consulting room entrance is at the back of the house, which means that the clients have to negotiate a rather complicated route that runs outside of my garden to reach it. Although I thought my instructions had been very clear the clients nevertheless failed to find me. I was waiting inside the house as I hadn't anticipated any problems and by the time I thought to look around the front of the house they were nowhere to be seen.

The couple telephoned to say that they had hovered on the green for about 10 minutes before calling it a day. In spite of my apologies for not having given clearer instructions they did not come back. When I told my supervisor, she suggested that in future I meet new clients on the street and guide them to my room. I took her advice and have been safely escorting new clients back to my consulting room ever since.

We need to remember that our clients are often ambivalent about beginning any sort of therapeutic work and that the tiniest of glitches can result in them deciding not to embark on the work with us.

I work at the top of a block of mansion flats and my clients have either to climb six flights of stairs or to take their chances with a very old fashioned lift. One day the inevitable happened and the lift, which always ascends the six floors alarmingly slowly, stopped and became stuck, mid floors. I called the fire brigade out, but they took about half an hour to arrive. I spent over half the session sitting on the floor conversing through the grating of the lift door to my client's disembodied head. Fortunately neither of us panicked.

We cannot always protect our clients from difficult situations.

The bell

It had taken me ages to pluck up the courage to go to see Mrs Alexander, but my friend had recommended her as a good psychoanalyst. We were getting on well when the front door bell rang. Without leaving her chair she pressed a button on the floor with her foot, which presumably opened the front door, I felt as if I was on a conveyor belt – no of course I didn't say anything to her, but I never went to see her again.

I imagine the analyst in question had many theories about why this client did not return for a second consultation, but I doubt her foot on the button was one of them. What was commonplace to her and an efficient way of responding to the bell without leaving her consulting room felt denigrating to this vulnerable client who was seeing the analyst for the first time.

If the analyst had been able to anticipate the effect her action would have on her new client she might have been able to reassure her by explaining, saying something such as, 'I don't like to leave you so I will let my next client in by pressing this button.' Although this might go some way to reassuring the client, I do not think it would necessarily remove the notion that the analyst had clients queuing up like planes over Heathrow. If we stress to clients the need to be more or less on time, it does remove the necessity to jump up to open the door, and gives the therapist and the clients the peace of mind that they will not be interrupted.

Many people come to our doors during the day and we need to decide how best to deal with unwanted intrusions. If you are working in a clinic or somewhere where there is a receptionist the problem is solved, but for those of us who are working from home it is more complicated. Two bells are a good idea: one for domestic use and one with your initials on it for your clients. This works well for me because I cannot hear the home bell when I am in my consulting room and therefore do not have the anxiety of deciding whether to ignore it or not. Just as if you were working away from home, you can make arrangements for deliveries and tradespeople to come when you are available to answer the door.

Do remember to tell the client which bell to ring.

Entrance hall

The way through to the consulting room needs to be as clear as possible. Your clients should not have to wade through an untidy clutter. If you have a family it may not be possible and you may not want to remove all signs of them, but try to have coat pegs free for your clients' use and make it all as tidy as you can.

If your consulting room is not on the ground floor I suggest that you lead the way up the stairs, having already made sure that all the rooms you pass have their doors closed. When you show your clients out, follow them down the stairs. This piece of advice was given to me by a therapist who had been pushed down the stairs by a very disturbed client. These decisions might seem incidental to the larger picture, but it is important when we are thinking of our container. If we have thought through our situation and are clear about such matters as showing clients to our consulting room, they will feel that we are taking good care of them and we will feel confident that we are able to look after both our clients and ourselves.

You might want to think about having a panic button if you are working in isolated conditions. I do not know of anyone who has one, but in some circumstances it might be worth considering.

The bathroom

If possible it is helpful to have a cloakroom that is used only for your clients while you are working. The lavatory must be clean with spare toilet rolls available, and a fresh hand towel should be by the wash-basin. It is also useful to leave a glass, so that if a client needs a glass of water you can point them to the cloakroom rather than having to leave the room to fetch them one. If your clients do have to use your personal bathroom it is important to do your best to make it as free as possible from lotions and potions. But think hard about creating a designated cloakroom for your clients. You can fit a toilet and washbasin into the tiniest of spaces and the waste can be pumped up from a basement if necessary. Think creatively. This may be your working environment for many years to come.

Quiet please, therapy in progress

Wherever the room is, it needs to be quiet, clean, private, airy and warm.

> I remember enduring a few sessions with my therapist that were blighted by terrible music from the room next door. Her consulting room was in a Victorian block of flats. It was a huge and delightful room and had been very quiet, so this onslaught came out of the blue. It was very distracting for me and I imagine terrible for her as she was there all day. However, we did not suffer for long, because after a few noisy sessions the room became quiet again. As I understood it negotiations had not worked so the shared wall was soundproofed.

To the best of our ability we need to ensure we have a quiet room. If it is on a busy street we can install double glazing; if we have noisy children we can have a double door, situate the room as far away as possible from potential noise, lay fitted carpet, soundproof a wall, muzzle the children, or see clients only while the children are at school.

All options, apart from muzzling the children, are possible and need to be considered before we decide where to see our clients. But what of the unexpected? Whether we are working in an urban or a rural environment we will be subjected from time to time to noise over which we have no control. Car alarms, sirens, drilling, builders, combine harvesters; the possibilities are endless and it is our job to keep the therapeutic space safe from intrusion and disruption.

When we cannot do anything about the noise, it is probably best to acknowledge the nuisance of it and remind yourself that you cannot be responsible for the outside world or control the universe.

But is it clean?

Cleanliness is less of a problem; all it requires is that we clean our room. It is remarkable that some therapists neglect this aspect of their environment.

> I was terrified of going to see a therapist. From hearsay I thought they were rather arrogant, but knew I had to do something about my depression. The meeting was as unnerving as I had feared and I absolutely hated feeling exposed and vulnerable, but what was really upsetting and convinced me that psychotherapy was not for me, was the state of the therapist's room. It was disgusting, there was an old coffee cup sitting on top of a heap of untidy papers on her desk and an overflowing waste paper basket in the corner. I felt as if this therapist had not prepared for me and really did not care whether I saw her again or not.

This woman might not have been a candidate for psychotherapy anyway, but what a pity that the room confirmed her prejudice that psychotherapists were an arrogant group who were interested only in theory not in people.

Sadly I do not think this experience is unusual. It can often be the case that we become careless of our environment and forget that what is familiar and homely to us can be a bewildering clutter to a new client who, of course, will say nothing but may vote with her feet and never return.

A breath of fresh air

A consulting room should be warm but also be airy. Who wants to work in a stuffy room? Indeed, how can we work in a stuffy room? We need oxygen to think and, dare I say it, stay awake. I trained in a wonderful institute but remember being amazed that our director, a marvellous woman of advanced years, not only smoked in her consulting room, but also smoked when she was seeing clients – impossible to imagine now. In fact it has been years since I have had a client ask if he could smoke. Occasionally a client arrives smelling of cigarettes, which is unpleasant, and it is important to freshen the room after he has gone.

No one must know I am here

Discretion is fundamental to good practice and it is up to us to ensure our clients' privacy to the best of our ability. This is particularly important if we are working at home. We might have found a suitable room to work in but be hard pressed to create a waiting room. So we need to think about how to manage our timing so that clients do not bump into each other. It is difficult to know what to do with a client who arrives early; a chair in the hall could possibly work, but only if the house is empty apart from you and if your clients can come and go without passing each other in the hall.

If we do not have a waiting room it is best to let the client know before their first visit. We can say something like, 'I am afraid I don't have a waiting room so it is helpful for us both if you don't arrive before time.' Best not to say, as a newly qualified counsellor reported to her supervisor, 'Please don't arrive before time because I cannot deal with you.' That makes it sound as if the client is a terrible burden who is going to need 'dealing with' by a counsellor who finds it hard to cope.

First impressions

First impressions are all-important, and it is most often the case that the first point of contact will be a telephone call. So much information is given and received before we have even met our clients: the sound of our voice, the message on the answerphone and then of course the first conversation.

It is really helpful to have a telephone dedicated to the practice. That way it can be on permanent answerphone, which means that you are never caught off guard and have time to think before responding to the call. It is useful to keep a notebook by the phone so that when you are listening to your calls you can jot down the date, number and any other information you have been given, such as who suggested they call, which is so useful to refer back to at a later date.

I recall being really surprised when I rang a very well-known therapist who answered the telephone in a cheerful and decidedly unprofessional way. It was refreshing to hear her voice, devoid of the formality that I was expecting from a therapist.

This therapist was clearly not particular about separating her professional and personal life, at least not as far as first impressions were concerned, but if you wish to be informal you need to be able to pull it off and I do not think the majority of us have that kind of panache – certainly not when we are first setting up in practice.

The all-important message on the answerphone should be short and to the point. We do not need to sound depressed as if anticipating the mood of our would-be client, and we should avoid sounding unduly caring and seductive. It is interesting to listen with a critical ear to voicemail messages: they all reflect something of the messenger. Suggest to the caller both that they let you have a couple of times when it would be convenient to call them back and that they leave their telephone number, but it is not necessary for you to acquire more information than that.

> The other day when I got the answerphone message of an experienced therapist I heard her ask not only for the caller's telephone number, but also the time of the call and address of the caller. I cannot think of any reason why she would need to know my address and asking for it sounded intrusive.

Your answerphone message and the way you deliver it will be unique to you and it is worth practising a bit until you are satisfied with it. Of course, the client's first impression of you may come from a website, which we address later.

The blank screen

Different aspects of our client's internal world of unconscious relationships will, from time to time, be projected on to his therapist and be made conscious through the work. To enable this process to take place an analytical psychotherapist will deliberately aim to be a blank screen. Whichever discipline we follow, we endeavour not to divulge details of our personal life.

However, it is impossible to present ourselves as a completely blank screen. From the state of the doorstep to the pictures on the wall, or indeed lack of pictures on the wall, we are saying something about ourselves. Freud's clients would have known of his interest in antiquity: his consulting room was full of artefacts that showed his interest in archaeology and much more.

How you furnish your room and what objects you introduce into it is a matter of personal taste. If your room is also your office you will need to find space for a computer, a telephone and probably a filing cabinet. You can neatly solve the tidiness problem by having a desk that can be closed up; it can be big enough to contain your laptop and a mass of papers and still look attractive. If you are very untidy you can solve the problem by putting the office equipment behind a screen.

If you are quite tidy you might prefer to have an ordinary desktop PC on your desk along with the telephone, which will be switched to off when you are seeing clients. You may be able to contain all your paperwork in drawers. If you have bookshelves I suggest they only contain professional books. It is probably reassuring to our clients to see that we have an arsenal of professional literature at our disposal, but best for them not to be able to judge us by the covers of our personal books.

There is no need for us to have photographs of friends and family in the room, and on the whole, if possible, it is best not to have too many signs of family life around. Our clients need to feel that we are there for them and the fewer signals they have of our personal life the better. It is important to create an atmosphere that you enjoy working in – after all, you will be spending many hours in this room – but there is a balance to strike between anonymity and familiarity, between dignified comfort and too much cosiness.

Our clients will be absorbing information about us from the moment they approach our front door; indeed, from the moment they saw our website or heard our voice on the telephone. But this should be about the professional us, uncluttered by the paraphernalia of our personal lives.

All professions demand integrity from their practitioners; that is what it means to be a professional. There is, I believe, an extra dimension for those of us who work with clients in such a personal and intimate way. The boundary between personal and professional is less obvious; there is less for us to hide behind, particularly when we work at home, so we need to endeavour to clear any distractions from our physical space just as we aim to clear the emotional and psychological clutter from our mental space.

What about us?

Just a quick word about us and the way we present ourselves. We owe it to our clients to look neat, be clean and to smell fresh. You would think that this would be a given, but therapists can be as careless with themselves and their appearance as they can be with their rooms, imagining perhaps that there is no need to pay attention to physical details when they are so fully engrossed with minds.

But why would you not want your therapist to look good? In some respects we are acting as a role model for our clients. We want our doctors to be healthy and we want our therapists to be personable. It does not say a great deal about the effectiveness of our work if we cannot take good care of ourselves, and it can show disregard for our clients if we look shoddy. All professions tend to have a characteristic look and if we work at home our look might be casual, but casual should not mean unkempt. Whatever your style, it will say a lot about you.

A shared room

There are many ways of working. When we are just starting out and do not have a full practice, it can help us financially to share a room with another practitioner. If we have our own consulting room we can rent it out for the hours we are not using it. If we have not managed to establish a consulting room of our own, we can search for a practitioner who has one and negotiate a number of hours a week to see clients there. We do sacrifice the flexibility of having a room available whenever we want it when we choose either of these options, but if we are worried about money then sharing space might be the best choice.

> I decided to stop working on one day a week and was fortunate to find a colleague, who was relocating for her husband's job and who needed to find a room in which to see a few remaining clients. The arrangement worked very well: I was glad of the extra income and my friend and colleague rented a room that was familiar and pleasant to work in. There was also an unlooked-for bonus in the arrangement, which was that I could not be persuaded to fit in an extra client on my day off as I had nowhere to see one. My free time was well protected.

If we choose to share our rooms, what are the options? If we want to rent our room out we can use word of mouth to let people know that we have spare capacity; we can advertise in the local professional directories; or we can use the various notice boards of our professional bodies. It is important to interview your would-be tenant and check out his credentials and draw up a clear agreement to suit you both. I suggest you do not commit yourself for more than a year, unless you are absolutely clear about how much you want to work. You might find yourself frustrated to have the work coming in and nowhere to do it.

Clinics, institutions and the NHS

You could decide that your best option is to work in a clinic, or there might be a suitable building in your area where rooms are rented out to therapists on an hourly basis. Often in these situations there is a receptionist who will take calls, a waiting room and suitable toilet facilities.

If you are not working in private practice, you may be working in an institution, a GP practice or with an agency. If so, it might not be possible to see clients in the same room each time. You may have little control over your working environment and the first connection clients have with you will possibly be with a receptionist or secretary.

There are pluses and minuses to working in a more public arena. The obvious lack of control over your working environment can be compensated for by having colleagues around you. Good management and secretarial help will offer containment for both you and your clients.

> I trained at a large institute in London and still blush when I remember taking in a geranium on my first day. I guess I was determined to make the place my own. I was lucky enough to share a room with a fellow trainee and although it was tiny and the furniture pretty basic, we managed to make it comfortable and attractive. The room became very much our own; in fact I remember a member of staff being incredulous that our space was the same as his and yet looked completely different, warm and inviting. Somehow four chairs and two desks were squeezed into this tiny room, hardly room to swing a cat, but we had a colourful rug, a decent picture on the newly painted wall, plants, including my geranium, on the sunny window sill, and our books on the shelves. We cleaned the windows and polished the furniture. Our names were on the door. It was our room and we loved it.

Some would find it easy to create a pleasing environment out of a concrete cell, others might require some help to do so, but we all have to work a little harder to create an inviting environment in which to see clients if we do not have a room of our own.

Sometimes we have no choice

I had decided after many years of working in the country to transfer my practice to a busy city. I have gone to a lot of trouble over the years to make my consulting rooms nice places to be, and the one I have in the country where I live is wonderful. One of my clients said, 'I feel better just walking into this room.' By contrast, the room I found to rent in the city is dark and somewhat depressing. It is in a basement of a busy doctor's surgery with not much natural light; it is distinctly scruffy, even grubby, and there are lots of yellowing papers pinned to the notice board. I was about to turn it down and then I thought, 'The counsellor who works here on other days has a busy and successful practice – and so do the doctors whose rooms are not much better, so what am I fussing about?'

I imagine that because this counsellor is long experienced she will be able to inspire confidence in her clients in spite of the poor surroundings, but there is much she could do to improve the rather dismal basement she finds herself in. She could clean the windows and polish the furniture, perhaps put a vase of fresh flowers on the desk. She might discuss the yellowing pieces of paper on the notice board with the therapist who shares the room with her and, if they are not of any importance, take them down and replace them with something cheerful and relevant to her client work. She could even decide to invest in the space by painting the walls. Furniture can usually be moved around to create a containing atmosphere. Remember the trainee therapists who created a delightful space out of the tiny room they were given.

Your room is a container for the work that you do, and over the years it will remain a safe and familiar place for both you and your clients. There are different demands for different therapies. A group therapist will need quite a large room. A child therapist might not need such a big space but it will have to accommodate toys and drawing materials and she will want to have blankets and pillows available and perhaps a soft rug on the floor. A family or couple therapist will need more chairs than the psychotherapist who only sees one client at a time. A psychoanalyst will usually include a couch in her room.

Whatever particular requirements you have, if you have thought carefully about your working environment and the needs of your clients it will be apparent to them. At an unconscious level they will feel held and contained; you will have created a physical and psychological space in which your clients can feel comfortable and able to trust whatever therapy you have to offer them.

> I can tell that you care about your clients, there is such a feeling of things being looked after. I cannot really explain it, but everything looks as if you have thought about it. My physical needs feel taken care of. I met an old friend the other day and we were reminiscing about the time when we were both in psychotherapy with the same person. It was years ago, but my friend asked me: 'Do you remember she never had any paper in the loo?'
>
> I did remember that, as well as the untidiness of the hall and that it could sometimes be quite cold in the consulting room. She was an excellent therapist, but I didn't feel that I had been prepared for, I didn't feel held in the way I do here. I think I have internalized something that is nurturing without even noticing.

We do not often have our efforts commented on, and it is probably rather unusual for a client to be as consciously aware of her surroundings as the woman in this anecdote, but unconsciously our clients will register that we have taken care to provide a warm, clean and secure environment for them. When they walk into our room they will feel that, just as in the previous week and the week before that, the space is ready for them, predictable and unchanged by time. Life outside may chop and change, but the consulting room remains the same, a safe container within which good work can be done.

2

The Clients

I found him on the internet under 'group therapies'. It was a
very good website and he seemed to be experienced so I didn't
drive myself mad trawling through therapist after therapist.
Interestingly, when I then mentioned his name to friends many
said they had heard that he was a very good therapist, I plumped
for him.

As the business of therapy becomes increasingly competitive it can feel a daunting task to get started and find work.
Even established therapists have their moments of anxiety when
their practice is low on clients. As we come to the question
of finding work we have much to consider and many options
open to us.

In the last chapter it became clear that it would be more difficult
to create your own unique environment if you were working in a
GP practice or agency than it would be if you were setting up a
practice in your own home. However, the reverse is true when it
comes to finding clients.

It can be an easier environment in which to find work if you
are attached to a medical practice or an agency. Customers are
not a problem if you are working for an established agency, which
will have a presence in the community, will constantly advertise
and will have a steady stream of clients. If you are working in a
GP practice the doctors will refer their patients to you. An agency
such as Relate usually has a waiting list.

Getting started

One option when you are first qualified is to align yourself to an established organization, institution or agency. You may already have had experience of working in an institution; many counselling and psychotherapy courses expect you to have found a placement in a school or counselling agency or other appropriate setting during your training. If you have enjoyed working in a particular organization you could negotiate to continue with them for a while; you might decide that working institutionally seems preferable to setting up on your own, at least for a short time.

Even if working for others is not your preferred option, to commit yourself to a few hours a week with an organization that is providing the clients can be really helpful. The knowledge that you are guaranteed some paid hours will make you feel more confident of finding private work and will also give you a ready-made group of colleagues.

> My local council offers free counselling sessions to members of staff, as does the university. I am a registered therapist with both organizations and regularly get referrals from them. They usually only pay for six sessions and it is part of my contract that I do not continue to see the clients after that, but I find it reassuring to know that I have a steady and regular source of work as well as my usual long-term clients.

Your training body may offer their graduates work. GP practices often employ one or two counsellors. Schools have student counsellors, as do universities. Hospitals employ counsellors. There are many ways of working outside private practice.

Some psychotherapy trainings find their graduates work for as long as they wish to be affiliated, and in return for the use of a consulting room and supervision the therapist agrees to work without receiving fees. Some of my supervisees have really enjoyed this way of working and continued for many years before deciding to set up their own practices.

You might decide to join agencies such as the Employment As-sisted Programme (EAP). The EAP acts as a service for company employees and will pay you direct on behalf of the client. Some churches also offer counselling referral services to their parishio-ners, and usually contribute to the cost of the sessions.

If you decide to work for an agency or in an institution the first contact a client has will usually be with the organization. In the case of the EAP the initial interview will be conducted by them. Setting up the meeting times, sorting out cancellations and billing will often be taken care of, which is liberating, but something can also be lost. When we have to negotiate those procedures ourselves, it helps us to make contact and engage with our clients at a fundamental level. There is nothing that keeps a new practitioner more on her toes than negotiating missed sessions and money with the client!

First impressions

Even if an agency has found us the work we still need to pay attention to the initial contact our client has with us and that all-important first session.

Although the agency will have dealt with the practical details of costs, and so on, it is important for the therapist to explain again to the client how things work. Really pay attention to what your client thinks about the practical arrangements and encourage him to express his feelings to you in the first consultation; he will then make the emotional and psychological contract with you, rather than with the agency.

> It was all such a long time ago, but I remember it so well. We had been married for about three months and after a terrible row with my husband – we had yet another sexual disaster – I knew I had to do something. I had heard of the Marriage Guidance Council and found their number in the telephone directory. It was quite out of

the question to expect my husband to go. I made an appointment with the receptionist over the phone and nervously turned up at the appointed hour to meet a counsellor. She seemed very nice, but when she asked about my father I was completely baffled as to why she wanted to know about him. At the end of the session I was asked if I wanted to contribute some money – I was utterly confused. I had no idea what was expected of me and I had no idea if I should go again.

No further appointment was suggested by the counsellor; I did not go back. A few years later I tried again to find someone to help me. This time I did more research. I asked around and a friend of mine recommended her counsellor; I had heard of him from other sources and knew he was an experienced man. Now I was less naïve and had more questions to ask him and I knew more about the counselling world. He told me what his fees were and explained how he worked. I felt reassured and less confused than I had on my first encounter with the marriage guidance counsellor, but I think my main reason for deciding to carry on seeing him was because my friend had said he was OK.

The Marriage Guidance Council is now Relate, and does not ask for contributions any more. Like everyone else they charge fees. It is also much more likely that our storyteller and her partner would go to see the counsellor as a couple, but the basic elements to finding and trusting a therapist, of whatever discipline, are still the same 30 years on. It is easy to forget that many people seeking help are confused and often distraught; that it might have taken a heroic effort just to find you, let alone trust and engage with you. I imagine our bride was terribly nervous when she saw the first counsellor and too shy to ask questions, but it also sounds as if the counsellor, while kind, did not understand how to contain her new client.

The second counsellor did have a head start: he had come recommended by a friend and was known in the area; but he took nothing for granted and contained his client; by letting her know, in the first session, what he charged and how he worked.

There was also the difference between working at an agency and working independently. The marriage guidance counsellor might have assumed that the agency had told the client what to expect, whereas the second counsellor had been the client's only contact from the first encounter.

It is important to remember that even if the initial contact and negotiations are made for us we must still forge our own contract, albeit a psychological one, with the client. In the case of the marriage guidance counsellor, she did not explain or make clear what counselling was all about, and failed to pick up and respond to her client's deep bewilderment.

Private practice

But you have decided to go it alone in private practice. You have your beautiful room, your professional telephone line in place, your stationery printed and friends and family put on notice of your new venture. Now you need clients!

Finding clients

With the increasingly sophisticated world of communications that we live in, we can no longer rely on just personal contacts to find new work, though for established therapists referrals will continue to be the most reliable and sustainable source. But it could be argued that even established therapists now need a presence on the internet, as many clients automatically search for a website in order to find out more about their would-be therapist.

Friends and family are contacts that many professionals can use when they first set up in practice, but we need to be cautious when the referrer is close to us; we need to keep our boundaries clear and start with a clean slate, as do our clients.

If you have been trained as a psychotherapist or psychoanalyst you will almost certainly have had a training patient, found through the training organization's referral system and you will probably have worked with the patient for some time before you graduated. Such patients may stay with you and become your first private clients as you move into private practice, which can be really helpful, as it means you will not be starting from scratch when you open for business.

Most psychotherapy trainings do not continue to find patients for their graduates, but they will have a referral service which you can join. If they do not then you could, together with other graduates, put together a proposal to start one.

Professional registers

The successful completion of your training will entitle you to register with your professional body. Most will have a register of practitioners and you will be entitled to add your name, telephone number, postal address and email address to it. This is a simple and straightforward task which begins to put you on the professional map.

There will also be more general registers; for instance, the British Association of Counsellors and Psychotherapists (BACP), or the United Kingdom Council for Psychotherapy (UKCP), which you may be entitled to join. You can ask for their criteria and, if you fit the bill, apply to be listed on their register of practitioners. These and other such bodies, which are well known to the public, are very useful to be attached to as they have a wide circulation and sound reputation. Usually you will be required to fill in a form each year to fulfil their professional requirements – a useful exercise for you and reassuring for clients.

What do you do?

If you do register with one of the more general registers you will be asked if you have any particular interests. This will allow you to specify your speciality, which will be helpful as, on the whole, people are seeking help for a particular problem and if they have turned to a register, perhaps unable to find a personal recommendation, they will be attracted to someone who shows an interest in their specific difficulties, such as bereavement or redundancy.

It can often happen that someone will ring up 'just wanting a bit of counselling'. In this case it is essential that you make clear to the caller that you will offer him an initial consultation to see if his problem fits your particular brand of therapy. It is tempting, particularly when you are just starting out, to take on anyone who approaches you. This is understandable in a way because you want the work and the money, but to take any case, regardless of the presenting problem, is not best practice either for the client or for your reputation.

Developing your reputation

It is much more professional, and ultimately more rewarding, to make it your business to be knowledgeable about who is in your professional community and who offers what – for example, adult/family/child/individual/couple therapy – so that if needs be you can refer your would-be client to the appropriate practitioner.

It might feel sacrificial to refer people on when you are trying to set up your practice, but ultimately it will bring rewards. You will come to find, know and gain the respect of your peer group, who ultimately will be an important part of your referral system.

When we have spent three or four years in training, we can become so familiar with our particular discipline that we imagine everyone must know how effective our work is and we might forget that most of us go about our daily business with little awareness of the working lives of other people. We need to let people know what we do in a clear and simple way.

I had been struggling to lose weight for years and none of the diets had been helpful. I would lose weight and then put it back on again. Someone suggested I went to see a counsellor and another suggested a nutritionist. Eventually I decided to see a counsellor. She was great; she asked me lots of questions not only about my eating habits but also about my childhood and present circumstances. For the first time I began to realize that my eating problem was emotionally based. The counsellor suggested another counsellor who specialized in eating problems. For the first time I felt hopeful that I might lose weight.

If I want to find an electrician or a plumber, I do not want to take pot luck by simply searching the web or looking in the *Yellow Pages*. I want, if possible, to have a personal recommendation. That is not really so difficult as everyone has at some time had to have their water, heating or electrical appliances fixed, and if my friends have happened upon a good tradesman they are usually only too happy to recommend them.

Therapeutic recommendations are not quite so easy. For those of us who work in the therapeutic community it does seem as if everyone knows someone who is a 'marvellous' practitioner, but many of our would-be clients do not have such helpful connections and will have to rely on the marketplace for their search. They are fortunate if they find someone who, in an initial consultation, has their best interests at heart; someone who will help them to decide what kind of therapy would be best for them.

Looking back at the therapies I have embarked upon, I find I did not shop around with any of them. I took the first one to come my way, rather than trying two or three before settling with one of them. That left me vulnerable in wanting to please, rather than deciding for myself who was or was not the right person.

In the first year or two, as you are building your reputation, you will not be able to rely as much on personal recommendations as you will when you have been in practice for a few years. In order to find clients you will need to put yourself about a bit – make personal contact with likely referrers – and be clear about what you are offering.

> There is absolutely no substitute for being a reliable, conscientious and hard-working therapist when it comes to building a successful practice. Ultimately the amount of work that we get will depend on our commitment to good practice and an intention and desire to do good work. If we are ambivalent about taking on the responsibility and rigour of seeing clients, our lack of commitment will be picked up, albeit unconsciously, and our practice will be unlikely to thrive.

Raising your profile

We have already identified ways of putting you on your particular therapeutic map. Make sure that you are on the appropriate register or registers for your particular discipline, as well as any general ones; these will both describe what you do and act as a good referral service network for you. Do make sure that your details are kept up to date.

It is helpful to have a leaflet printed that you can leave in GP practices and other useful places. I would suggest that you keep your message brief and your details clear – it needs to be professional and unfussy.

You can give copies of your leaflet to colleagues and friends; it is often easier for friends to hand someone written information, rather than to find a way of suggesting they consult you on the basis that they know you personally.

If there is a local directory of therapists in your area you could place a small advertisement in it. These are often free, but again you need to make sure the advertisement reflects the sort of therapy that you do, and err on the side of restraint. A good qualification is worth a thousand flowery words.

The *Yellow Pages* can be a useful way of advertising and, like other directories, will probably canvass you for business from time to time. Give all these possibilities some thought before you spend your money; the rewards might not justify the expense.

The website

It seems that most organizations and practitioners now have a presence on the internet and that, even if our clients do not use the net as a way of finding us, they will almost certainly check the internet to verify our credentials. Many of us who have been practising for years are reluctant to invest in a website, groan at the complexities and expense of building one and might worry about raising our profile so publicly, but whether you are just starting your career or have been practising for years it can be a very worthwhile investment.

Remember that if someone is trying to find a therapist from the internet, he will be seeking help for a particular problem rather than help from a particular person.

> I think a lot of people in relationships instantly think of going to Relate and don't really think much deeper about what therapy actually is or isn't – in that regard I guess a good starting point is to think what people really want, or think they are going to get, when they come to therapy, which will really change how they go about finding someone. They will obviously look under the heading of 'weight problems' if they want a dietician and under 'marriage breakdown' if they want a marital therapist.

Your website need not be elaborate – in fact, it is better if it is not – but it does need to be clear, letting the viewer know what it is that you do and how to get in touch with you. You can have appropriate links to any organizations you belong to, and include your publications. If you have an email address alongside your telephone number, you might suggest they telephone you in the first instance. You will be able to gain much more information from your potential client over the telephone than by email.

Take a look at a few websites to get some ideas. If you are at all adept at using the internet there are many businesses that offer you inexpensive ways of setting up a web page, but if you are not technically adept, it is worth investing in a professional designer. It is arguably better to have no website than one that looks amateurish.

Whichever way you decide to raise your profile the same rules apply: keep it simple, clear, precise and professional.

First encounters

To return to 'first impressions' which I mentioned in Chapter 1, your first encounter with a new client will most likely be on the telephone. They may have been referred, or found you themselves, but this initial conversation will be their first 'meeting' with you. They will already have formed an impression of you and the work you do by looking at your website, or listening to your voicemail message, but now they will be having a first-hand experience and, whether they realize it or not, will be taking in an enormous amount of information about you.

You, of course, will be taking in an enormous amount of information about them too; you might even be making brief notes as they speak. They may be very distressed and want, without any preamble, to make an appointment to see you as quickly as possible, or they may launch into telling you their whole problem, giving you little space to interrupt; they may have a thousand questions, or none at all.

If they ask practical questions about your fees, working hours or availability, you can quite briefly and straightforwardly answer them, but it is better not to get into a long discussion about their problem. You can say something like, 'I can understand that you are feeling upset, but I suggest we meet for an initial consultation when we can think more deeply about your situation.' In other words, it is more containing to acknowledge that you have heard the distress and move on than it is at this stage to listen, albeit sympathetically, to a long and complicated story.

It might be a simple telephone call that requires little more of you than a pleasant response, a discussion about a time to meet and directions, or the caller could be very demanding and need you to simultaneously hear his distress and impart practical information to him.

For these reasons many therapists never answer their practice telephone immediately. They let the answerphone pick up the first call, which means that when they telephone back they are prepared.

Engaging with the client

I was in a real dilemma. My children had just left home and I knew it was time to pick up a career again. I had lost all my old business contacts and anyway wasn't at all sure that I wanted to do the same thing as I had before; I wanted to try something new, but what? I saw an advertisement for careers advice in the local newspaper and seeing that the address was a very well-known clinic close to where I live I decided to give it a try. It was the most distressing hour I have ever endured. The psychoanalyst, for that was what she was, treated me as if I were a patient; she paid scant attention to the careers problem, focusing instead on my children leaving home, my husband's high-powered job and what she described as my envy of the children! I felt humiliated and utterly distraught and cried for hours when I got home.

What a sorry tale. The psychoanalyst may well have been accurate in her understanding of the client's psychology but she had not been given permission to analyse this client, who had responded to an advertisement for careers counselling.

This client may well have had emotional problems that were being exacerbated by her children leaving home, and if an alliance had been forged between her and the analyst in the first consultation it might, in due course, have been helpful and possible to delve further into the situation the client found herself in. As it was, the clinic was offering careers counselling – and that was the remit of the consultation.

The upshot of this unfortunate encounter was that the clinic lost a client and the client lost an opportunity to sort out her career. She also decided never to seek any sort of psychological help again, another unfortunate consequence of this non-therapeutic encounter.

Meeting

At the first consultation a meeting takes place between a couple wanting a solution to their problem and a couple-therapist who has psychotherapy to offer them. Two very different views of the world therefore sometimes meet in the first consultation and, when a decision is made at the end of the assessment process to continue to

work together, this is because some kind of marriage has been made between those different conceptions – the idea of a marital problem and the idea of therapy.

Although this was written with couple psychotherapy in mind, we can extrapolate it to apply the thinking to any practitioner who is meeting a client for the first time.

A fee-paying client

Given that the transition from first contact to first consultation has gone well, that your directions have worked, that the client has found the house and accessed the right door, has not tripped over the cat, has found a hook to hang his coat on and is now safely seated in your quiet, clean, comfortable and airy consulting room, all that is left is for you to engage with him and convert him into a fee-paying client.

Your client will have both conscious and unconscious expectations of this first meeting. It may have taken him weeks to come to the decision to see you, and if your client is a couple they may be arriving from completely different places, both geographical and psychological. You may find that you cannot get a word in edgeways or you may find that your client is speechless. He may be very clear about his symptoms or just be vaguely aware that 'something feels wrong'.

If we go back to the notion of a 'marriage taking place' between you and the potential client, you may both have a different perception of the first consultation. You might be thinking of the meeting as an assessment to see if you can work with this person or persons, perhaps wondering if the client has found the right therapist for the problem. You will also be trying to gain as much information as possible, while acknowledging whatever emotional pain they might be in. You will also want to discuss the practicalities of the way you work.

The client will be in a different place, perhaps overwhelmed by his problem, possibly frightened of what he might be embarking on, maybe bewildered. He might be too distressed to take anything in, or having finally got to you, taken a flight into health resulting in his feeling that the visit is unnecessary.

You may decide that the way you want to manage the initial assessment/consultation is to have a longer than usual session, say an hour and a half instead of an hour, or you could think that offering the possibility of two consultations to your clients will allow more time for reflection. How you choose to work is your business and your decision, but you must make it clear to your client what you are offering and why.

> I like to offer my clients, who are usually couples, the possibility of two consultations as it gives me time between the two sessions to think about the initial consultation and the problems as presented. I explain to my clients that two initial consultations gives us all a chance for reflection and an opportunity for them to ask me questions and see whether they feel they can work with me or not. If it is quite obvious that the clients do not want a second consultation and want to get going immediately, it is fine. I do not insist on a second consultation.

It may be the case that a client wants to start therapy immediately or seems to need more than two consultations before he can decide whether to commit himself to therapy. Whatever the circumstances, if you take your time and respond to the situation and needs of the client as they present themselves, so that the client feels truly 'heard', 'a marriage will be able to take place' between what you have to offer and what the client needs and wants.

Some clients may ask how you work, where you were trained, or how long you have been qualified, while others might not have the slightest interest in you or your qualifications, but the purpose of the initial consultation is to allow for questions to be answered if they arise. It is a chance to discuss fees, your policy on holidays, whether you charge for missed sessions and any other factors that are going to impact on the progress of the therapy. For instance, if you do not have a waiting room this will be the time to ask your clients not to arrive early and to tell them why.

Whether you expect that the client will be with you for a long time or for just a few sessions, it is really helpful that the client knows what is in your mind, how you are thinking about his problem and what he should expect from you. It is an opportunity to make clear what the contract, albeit informal, is between you. You might decide to follow up the discussion of practical arrangements with a letter, or decide that a clear discussion is enough.

Whatever conclusion you come to, it will be clear that you have taken the trouble to think through both the practical and the psychological aspects of the first meetings. Your thoughtfulness will be apparent to your client; he will feel met by you and held by you. You have engaged a new customer. You are in business.

3

Money Matters

How do I know how much to charge? Well, I look out of the window as they arrive; see what type of car they are driving and charge them accordingly.

Money and the so-called caring professions make uneasy bedfellows, and the newly qualified graduate will, all too often, have had little or no instruction on how to manage the financial side of her business We need to be realistic and accept that, while we have chosen to work in the caring and helping professions, we are nevertheless working within an increasingly competitive world of therapeutic practitioners. Although our reasons for training may not have been primarily based on a desire to make money, most of us do need to make a living out of our professions. We should not be squeamish about acknowledging this.

As part of my training I was required to attend a weekly clinical workshop which consisted of both students and members of staff. Each week the students would present one or two ongoing cases for the group to discuss. I really enjoyed these case discussions, in fact they were probably one of the most helpful features of my training. I learned to listen carefully to the material presented without forming premature opinions about the client's problems and without judging them on their position in society, their sexual orientations or race. Whatever the clients were struggling with, the workshop members treated them with respect, often digging deep into their compassionate and professional selves in order to comprehend the incomprehensible; but there was one prejudice that often went unchecked: an unconscious contempt for the businessman.

We would not be judgemental about the colour of our client's skin and we should not be judgemental about the colour of their money. Money, whether we like it or not, makes the world go around and it is an important factor in the business of setting up and maintaining a practice.

Sex therapists are spared no blushes during their training when they are expected to recognize and be able to speak to the difference between an erect or semi-erect penis, but as far as I know there is no such training associated with understanding and speaking to the state of our client's bank accounts. I remember the relief of a client of mine, who had made a lot of money in property, when I asked him just how much money his deal had brought him. It seemed I was the only person he could discuss his good fortune with, he was so frightened of people's envy.

> Some years ago I attended a weekly professional experiential group where I was the only member not from the medical or therapy professions. My profession is accountancy and my concerns are the money matters of a mixed bag of hundreds of individual clients. My repressive, guilty, unspoken sex education was gleaned from 'naughty' references in the Bible, newspapers and encyclopaedias. For months I squirmed in isolated, acute, hot discomfort in the group, as the medics calmly and clinically discussed orgasm, rape, masturbation and every type of perversion. The tables turned, however, when the theme changed to money and earnings. Suddenly I was the only one at ease in the group; while everyone else fidgeted, mumbled and fumbled to avoid their money secrets being aired, I became confident and realized that I was the sole exception to the rule, that the vast majority would rather discuss incest than income.

How do I know how much to charge?

We certainly do not want to base our fees on the value of our client's cars, but it can be difficult to determine how much to charge when there are few official guidelines to help us. Unlike many professions, such as the law or medicine, the therapeutic world has no published rate of earnings to call upon. This leaves the private practitioner with the dilemma of where to set their financial bar; however, there are many yardsticks, both economic and social, to help us reach the all-important decision of how to pitch our fees.

Many of us will have had our own analysis or psychotherapy, which will give us an idea of what experienced clinicians charge, and we will no doubt have a supervisor who will also be billing us. We can ask around our recently qualified peer group, and members of any professional group or society that we belong to, to find out what they are charging their clients, but in my experience fee levels are rarely a topic of conversation among therapists; there is a certain reticence in talking about money in general and personal fees in particular.

I have always run a 'Robin Hood practice' as I am reluctant to turn patients away because they cannot afford my fees, I might lose some really interesting patients from whom I could learn a lot, if I remain stubbornly attached to a rigid fee scale. So if I think my patient might not be able to afford my standard fee, or if I feel that the effort of managing to pay will interfere with the therapeutic work, I will negotiate with them and adjust the fee accordingly.

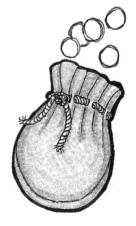

This writer is a psychoanalyst and she highlights an important aspect of her work. Unlike many professionals, such as a lawyer, accountant or physiotherapist, she will be offering to her clients ongoing long-term analysis. She might feel that sessions twice or even three times a week would be of great benefit to her patient and need to take that into account when she is negotiating the fee. This is a quite different situation from that of a counsellor who might be offering short-term work of, for example, 20 weeks. It is quite easy for a client to budget for 15 weeks' work, another matter entirely to commit himself to long-term open-ended therapy – with possibly more than one session a week; such clients might be committing themselves to paying the equivalent of a medium-sized mortgage.

> It is a trade-off between the work I want to do, economics and what I can afford.

So if we choose to do long-term analytic work we will need to think what that will mean economically. Can we afford to run a practice that requires us to do many more client hours than a practitioner who works less intensively and charges his clients more? The justification for charging more if you are seeing clients only once a week is that it is more difficult to hold 20 clients in mind than it is to hold 10 clients in mind who you are seeing twice a week, or seven patients for three sessions a week.

A psychoanalyst who worked 45 hours a week to support three growing boys admitted that she could only do so because she saw many patients two or three times a week. She enjoyed the intensive work and charged modest fees, but gave herself the incentive of seeing patients once a week as well, by charging them more.

What can the market bear?

You need to know what type of clients you might expect to have and what your peer group is charging. If you are working in central London you are more likely to have affluent clients than if you are working in the suburbs or a small town. The psychoanalyst who worked 45 hours a week had a practice that consisted of social workers, teachers and people who commuted daily into London. Not high flyers or high payers. By contrast, one of her colleagues who worked in central London charged twice as much as she did. Market forces play just as big a part in a therapist's world as in any other.

Seniority and effectiveness should be a factor in determining what we charge, but it often is not. I know many very experienced psychotherapists who charge far less than someone who has just finished their training. Sometimes a newly qualified therapist will charge a high fee because they do not want to appear inexperienced and a novice; and practitioners who have been working for years charge too little because they become out of touch with a peer group, many of whom might have retired.

I heard of two therapists who decided from the outset that they would run their practice as a business. They created a marvellous website, gave their 'therapy business' a name, rented a room and borrowed money as a float. This of course meant that they needed to charge high fees from the outset. It worked for them as they were very clear about what they needed to charge in order to be successful. I guess they knew their market.

So you have the example of your mentors, supervisors, your own therapists and any work experience you have had, and you have checked with your peer group to see what fees they are charging. You have an idea of the clientele you are likely to have; you know what market forces operate in your area; you know what you need to earn and you have squared that with the work you want to do. You may be the only breadwinner and responsible for a family, or only have yourself to look after; you could have decided to work part time or be subjecting yourself to a punishing regime. However, you have decided to structure your work; having thought about it you will be able to discuss and negotiate your fees with confidence. Never underestimate the value of 'thinking': thinking is containing, both for you and your client.

Reviewing your fees

Once you have decided what you are going to charge your clients it is important to remember that they might be with you for some time and that you will need to review your fees from time to time. As we saw in the last chapter, the first consultation will be an opportunity to let your new clients know the practical details of how you work; these should include the fact that from time to time you will review your charges. It will do no harm for those clients who will not be with you for long, and it will be a crucial piece of information for clients who you could be working with for years. It will help you enormously when the time comes to put up your fees if you have notified your clients in advance that you might do so. But reviewing fees need not mean putting them up; they might remain the same or, in some cases it might be best practice to reduce them.

> I sometimes say to my patients that I have reviewed my fees and decided that this year I will keep them the same, but will review them again in a year's time. I know I am giving them the impression that I am a nice therapist by not putting my fees up and that I am therefore preparing the ground for the following year when I could be regarded as a less kind therapist by increasing them.

What a curse consciousness can sometimes be! Our 'nice' therapist, by confessing to a tiny manipulation of events, is highlighting just how difficult it can be to raise our fees.

No matter how conscientious we are, most of us cannot help but have a practice that has a wide range of charges. Even if we do a review once a year and increase the fees by a small amount, we might still need to start a new client at an altogether higher rate in order to keep pace with the outside world. Juggling with these complex issues is a vexed and lonely business, but many of our clients who have money worries feel that we are above such mundane matters and not interested in their financial problems;

we can prove them wrong by analysing and taking seriously our own attitude to money.

To be able to speak to your client about his finances without feeling intrusive or embarrassed is as important as being able to mention his sexual problems, envy or rage, all of which we learn to be comfortable with. If you are feeling confident about the way you charge and can justify an increase of fee, it will not necessarily stop your client from having a reaction when you do it; after all, none of us likes to pay more for anything than we already are, but it is far better to claim authority for your action than hand the authority to someone else.

I had been seeing this wonderful counsellor for some time, I really liked and trusted her, but when she put up her fees by a lot and told me it was because her accountant said she had to, I was furious. It was not that I minded her putting up the fees, although it was a big increase, it was that she was being cowardly by hiding behind her accountant. It was a shame because my view of her really changed – and not for the better.

Billing

When I started my training I was given an academic diary; I now have a stack of them in different glorious colours reminding me of the very many years that I have been in practice. The diary consists of a double page per week, and in the back are several pages of graph paper. This combination is all I need to record who I have seen, whether they kept their appointment or not, how much they owe me, when I billed them and if they have paid me. Obviously my diary contains the names and times that my clients are due, but it contains much more. In the back of the diary using the graph paper, I record all the practical details of the sessions. I give each client a column putting the dates they are due and the amount they pay for each appointment in the little squares. I can then easily record whether they have kept their appointment with me or not by placing a tick or a cross in the little square. At the end of the month I add up the amount due, record the date I gave the client the bill and put a circle around it when they have paid me.

Simple! Some of my colleagues are at home with accounting programs on their computer and I know many therapists who use hand-held computers to record times of sessions. I hear of complex and idiosyncratic methods that my friends swear by, but I have never seen a system that is more efficient than mine!

It does not matter what method you use to record sessions, billing and payments as long as it is clear to you and easy to manage. The advantage of this system is that recording the sessions, amount due and payment made is immediate and close to hand.

There are different ways of billing your clients. You might use a compliments slip, simply handwriting the amount due. You can order invoices from a printer or create your own on your computer, printing several off when you need them. If you choose to create your own, try A5 paper, putting your name and address at the top, plus telephone number and email address; a little further down print 'To' followed by line spaces where you will insert the client's name. The amount of money due can be written under, 'For Professional Services'. There will be room at the bottom to print 'Date', to which you can add the appropriate date to the invoicing of your client.

If you are seeing a client for ongoing work, it is efficient to bill them on a once-a-month basis, but if, for example, you are doing two initial consultations you might decide to bill separately for those two sessions. If you are not working in such a structured way, it might be best to bill your client after each session. Some clients insist on paying each time they come, even if they are in regular therapy.

How do I manage my billing? Simple: I earn fees in month one; bill the first week of month two, and allocate the money in month three.

Whatever method you decide to use, it is important that both you and your client are clear about it. If you are invoicing at the end of the month, be consistent. I give my clients a bill on their last session of the month and I put the bill under a little wooden duck on the small table beside them. If the client does not pick it up, I point it out to him before he leaves. If I am in a process of consultations with the client and we have decided on two or three appointments before he decides whether he will continue to see me on an ongoing basis, I will tell him that I will bill him at the end of the consultative process. The rule you adopt should be no surprises; your client needs to know what the score is, what you charge and when you will issue them with a bill.

Payment

It is crucial that, whatever method you are using, you keep an up-to-date record of money owed. If you are paid by cheque, make a note of the client's name in the paying-in book; you cannot be too careful when it comes to the dynamic between money and clients. If for some reason, which might be psychological, a client has not paid, then you need to be sure of your facts so that you can explore the matter from a strong position.

> Payments over the years have ranged from crumpled old notes thrown onto the table to pristine white envelopes with my name beautifully crafted on cheque and envelope: personally I prefer the former – it is all there on the table.

A few clients will want to pay in cash. I know that many therapists object to this and can feel uncomfortable about it. It can be difficult and embarrassing to maintain your therapeutic stance when money is being counted out before your eyes; and it may be the case that the client is being rather denigrating of the work that you do, but it might also be this particular client's way of dealing with money or it might be that he is anxious about there being enough money in the bank to pay you.

Whatever it means, you will take your time to find out, and if needs be, make an interpretation, but in the meantime you need to deal with the cash. If the client does not count the money out in front of you but hands you an envelope, it is best, particularly if you do not know him well, to count the money yourself. Difficult, I know, but what do you do if he has short-changed or overpaid you? If he has left before you realize the error, it will be your word against his. I have never been asked for a receipt, but should you be, you can simply write 'paid with thanks' on your invoice.

More and more clients are now asking if they can pay by electronic transfer, and I am occasionally asked if I take cards. I think it is perfectly reasonable to refuse to take cards, but I do think as time goes on we will need to embrace the electronic transfer, as for many the chequebook is becoming obsolete.

If you are going to accept electronic transfers it is a good idea to have an account dedicated to just this. Ask your clients to add their initials to the entry so that you can see at a glance whether a client has paid or not, and check the account regularly. You will need to decide at what point you will speak to the client if his payment is not recorded on your statement.

Difficulties can arise when the client is not paying for the sessions himself. When an organization, such as a church or workplace, is funding the counselling you need to be very clear about the method of payment. If possible it is most effective if the client can take responsibility for the transaction himself; that is, he collects the bill, gives it to the organization, and makes sure it is paid. However, this is not always acceptable to the company which is paying, in which case it is up to you to do the chasing. This can be time-consuming and frustrating, but the comfort of being on a register that feeds you work from time to time might well outweigh the frustration of having to chase them for payment.

The task can also become complicated when parents are paying for their teenage child to have therapy. The parents might then feel they have an involvement in the therapy, and even think they have a right to know what is going on. It is best in these cases to deal only with your client: give him the bill, and make it clear that you expect him to bring the cheque the following week.

Unpaid bills

My client had suffered terrible abuse; he sought help from me because both his domestic and business life were suffering because of his anxiety, which was the legacy of his awful childhood. He had little money available for therapy so I negotiated a reduced fee which he paid for six months. He then said that he was temporarily out of funds and asked if I would wait to be paid until the following month when he would be able to pay me. I agreed. The fees were not paid the following month, or the month after that. In fact I saw this client for another eight months without being paid. He finally left, promising to pay my bill just as soon as he could. Two years on, he has still not paid me.

> I feel there is nothing I can do to recuperate the money owing to me but I feel angry and let down. My good intentions have been abused.

I do not know of any therapist who has taken a client to court for non-payment. It would be unthinkable to do so. It is, therefore, up to us to make sure that we do not find ourselves in the position that this therapist did.

It might have been better for both this therapist and her client if she had been able to discuss the financial circumstances, and the impact these were having on her. But she was caught up by the deprivation her client had suffered and did not see that, by not paying her, he was acting out the abuse of his childhood.

Holidays and missed sessions

You have given a lot of thought to the difficult matter of how much to charge, you have a system set up to receive payment, and you are prepared to bite the bullet and review your fees yearly. It is now time to turn your attention to the breaks in your routine.

It does not really matter what your policy is as long as you can speak clearly to it, back it up with your logic, be prepared to argue the toss over it and have agreed it with your client before you start working with him.

> A charming man was referred to me by a colleague and friend of mine. He breezed into my consulting room, sat down in the chair and looked as if he had come to stay. His problem was immediate and pressing and I did my best to contain his anxiety. He told me that he had therapy many years ago with a therapist who had since retired; he now had to find someone else and I seemed to be that person. Each time I pointed out that he needed to know more about the way I worked, which might be different to his past experience, he dismissed my suggestion by saying, 'any friend of Anne's is good

enough for me – I completely trust her'. I gave up, but at the end of the session, in which I was able to gain an understanding of his problem, I said that I needed to let him know some practical details. I began by explaining that we would see each other once a week at the same time and that I charged for missed sessions. Suddenly my charming client exploded: he could not possibly work with such an inflexible person; his previous therapist had not worked like that, she had responded to his need for flexibility, as for paying for missed sessions . . . ! I never saw him again.

How important it was that the therapist was not seduced by this man's charm and accepting attitude. By insisting that she inform her new client of her working practice, she discovered the client's difficulty with commitment and boundaries.

Although this client's problem had been understood by the therapist, there was nothing she could do about it. Without a contract for regular sessions in place, a working alliance could not be forged. If a working alliance was not established it was not possible to define, understand and work with the presenting problem. It was the presenting problem that was preventing the client from engaging in ongoing therapy. It was a chicken and egg situation.

This highlights the subtle but important difference between setting up the work and doing the work. We must bring our business selves and therapeutic selves together in order to set in place the framework that will allow the often very hard and challenging work of therapy to take place. It is up to us to manage that balance, and while paying close attention to the problem that is being presented to us, make sure that the client has all the information he needs about our working practice.

Holidays

One of the advantages of working for oneself is being able, at least to some degree, to have a schedule that suits your particular circumstances. If you have children at school and decide to work only in term time for example, your holidays will reflect your clients' needs if they also have children of school age, but will not coincide with those of clients who do not, and who want to take advantage of cheaper holidays during term time. Whatever you decide, you certainly will not please all your clients when you publish your holiday policy.

> I am fortunate as I am not the only breadwinner in the family. When my children were small I aimed to work for about 42 weeks a year, which meant that I took a week or ten days off at Christmas and Easter; about five weeks in the summer and a half term to coincide with the school half terms in the spring and autumn. I tried to have my schedule sorted and available for clients by September. From time to time I have varied this pattern, but always come back to the familiarity of school holidays, even though I no longer need to. I like to have a rhythm to my working year. It suits me and many of my clients, but suits less those who like to take advantage of cheaper holidays out of season.

It is helpful, if your policy is to charge your client if his holidays do not coincide with yours, that you stick to a predictable holiday schedule. When circumstances demand more flexibility it is sensible to respond positively and try to work out a compromise. For instance, if a client is going to be away for longer than a month, but wants you to keep his time for him, you might decide to negotiate some sort of holding fee.

One of my supervisees operates a system that takes into account her complicated family situation. She has children on different continents who she visits at odd times of the year that do not usually coincide with UK holidays. She acknowledges this by not charging her clients for three weeks of their vacations over and above the times when she is away. For any further breaks the clients might take she asks them to pay half the fee.

There can be great differences between therapists in the way they manage their breaks, which reflect the varied circumstances of their working lives, but we must make sure, as part of our professional working contract, that our clients know what to expect of us; they can then choose whether to engage with us or not.

Missed sessions

I always charge for missed sessions and am quite prepared to justify my reasons for doing so, but I have just said goodbye to a patient who I saw for many years and I believe the analysis only succeeded because I was prepared to step outside my usual method of working. My patient often worked abroad; each time a business trip came up he would tell me that he had to go away and follow up his statement up with 'so that's it – that is the end of my therapy'. I was determined to challenge my patient's belief that if he could not keep his appointments with me I would give up on him. I managed, by being available to work on the telephone, by cutting down the sessions to one instead of two a week, and by not charging for some of the prolonged periods when he was away, to hold onto a belief that in spite of all the disruptions, we could continue to work together. If I had stuck determinedly to my usual practice I doubt that I would have been able to hold this patient. As it was he stayed for six years, eventually finding happiness with a partner in what is proving to be his first long-term relationship.

What might have been unhelpful and felt to be without boundaries for most patients proved to be an invaluable experience for this patient. No one had ever adjusted to his needs before and he truly believed that if he went away his therapist would give up on him. She maintained her belief in the work they were doing. Tenacity paid off.

Sometimes it is difficult for our clients to understand why we charge for missed sessions, particularly if they give us plenty of notice of an impending absence. Once again: if we have been clear about our policy on missed sessions at the start of therapy, we will find it easier to deal with any resistance to paying for them at a later date.

We are offering our clients a guaranteed, reliable presence for as long as it takes, which underpins a belief that no good work can be done unless we provide the all-important predictable and safe space for our clients. Our clients can be as disagreeable to us as they like, but they know that we will still be there for them the following week. If they choose to express their fury by missing a session it is of no matter; it is their session to use or not as they see fit. If we are seeing couples, they know that no matter how horrible they are to each other the session will be there for them to use the following week.

The contract between the therapist and the client ensures that the session is the client's; they have paid for it, and until an agreement is reached to end the therapy that time belongs to the client.

Charging for missed sessions has nothing to do with why the session is being missed. I had a client who didn't attend two sessions because of an ectopic pregnancy. I felt sympathetic and considered for a moment that I shouldn't charge her. Then I thought, how could £100 compensate for a lost baby! I kept to my policy.

You might agree with your client at the start of the work that if for some reason he could not manage to keep an appointment, you would try to change the session to another day in the same week. But it is best to leave yourself some wriggle room by stressing that if sessions were being changed on a regular basis you would want to explore why. You could choose to have an arrangement that allows your client to cancel a session without incurring a fee if he gives you 24 hours' notice – the flexibility that this arrangement allows can sometimes suit both therapist and client alike.

I am torn between feeling that what might seem rigidity may actually be containing and feeling that a bit of flexibility is human. I just could not bring myself to charge someone for going to a funeral of a close relative, but realize that this is a bit of a slippery slope that can end up with me making value (and moral) judgements. I remember, for instance, allowing my client to cancel, without a charge, when he needed to go away for training, but not for an extra-marital affair. I was, quite rightly, challenged on being morally judgemental.

Good practice

Most of us enjoy the work that we do; I doubt that we could do it if we did not. We give a lot of unpaid time and energy in supporting our professional societies; we invest in regular supervision for our clinical work, and maintain our professional standards by attending conferences and seminars as part of a need for continuing professional development. It is equally good practice to invest in an understanding of the part that money plays in our lives and in the lives of our clients.

4

Paperwork

If we listen very carefully on a Sunday morning we will hear, against the pealing of the church bells, the harmonious sound of a hundred therapists groaning as they reluctantly settle down to do their paperwork.

We have a matrix of professional relationships at hand to support and help us when we feel overwhelmed by our clinical work, but we can feel less supported when it comes to the more practical matters.

Most of us do not have an office separate from our consulting room, but we do have much of the paraphernalia that is usually housed in one. All businesses accumulate paperwork and the business of therapy is no exception. We must have insurance, pay our taxes, adhere to professional standards and maintain a professional profile. We can sometimes feel overwhelmed and ill equipped to cope with these demands, which are so removed from the nature of our work, but we need to keep abreast of these practical tasks and address such issues in order to sustain good professional practice and a successful business.

Stationery

A group of us who trained together decided, on graduation, to have business cards printed. We were thrilled to be setting up in practice and the cards were a symbol of our newfound professional status.

I don't know about my fellow colleagues, but I still have almost all those cards, now yellowed with age, stashed away in a drawer some 20 years later.

You might like to have some cards and, unlike this therapist, give them to colleagues, friends and other interested people. They will need to include your name, qualifications, telephone number and email address; you might want to add your website address if you have one.

You will need invoice paper; A5 is a good size to use, and envelopes to match. It is also useful to have A5 paper with just your name at the top. You will also need A4 paper with your name, address, telephone number and email address in the header and any professional memberships in the footer. Do not forget suitably sized envelopes. A simple white A6 card with your name and address stretched across the top is very versatile and can be used for all sorts of brief communications. It works as a compliments slip and a calling card. You can have your notepaper printed professionally or do it yourself; either way, it is good to have a stock in hand.

Keep tidy

One good filing cabinet should suffice to keep all the information you need to run your therapy business efficiently. An accumulated pile of undifferentiated paper left in a corner will rapidly become overwhelming, increasing your reluctance to sort it out. If you process it regularly, are rigorous and throw away pamphlets and periodicals you know you will never read, you will be left with a manageable amount of paper which you can file for future reference.

Referral systems

As your practice progresses, you will make many contacts with other therapists through professional activities and through client referrals. You will have contact with GPs, psychiatrists, social workers and colleagues from different disciplines, and over time you will develop an invaluable professional network. If you formalize your contacts by putting their names, contact numbers and an *aide-mémoire* on a card you will find over time that you will create a great resource for yourself.

Professional letters

During the course of a busy practice you will, from time to time, find it necessary to write a professional letter. If a GP or psychiatrist has referred a client, it is a matter of courtesy to let them know if the client has agreed to work with you. You might be worried about a vulnerable client and want to let his GP know that you are going to be away. You may see a client for an initial consultation and decide to refer him to someone else, in which case you will want to send your notes to the therapist you are referring him to. In all cases it is important to ask for the client's permission and to let him know what you intend to write; trust requires transparency.

Fear of suicide must be taken seriously, and even if a client refuses you permission to contact anyone, you would be failing in your professional duty if you did not contact his GP, but who tells what to who must be made clear to the client.

Writing a succinct and informative letter, which combines respect for the confidential aspect of your work, with giving sufficient information to the recipient, is a difficult business, and you might need to make several attempts at writing your letter before you are satisfied that you have achieved the right balance.

Professional notes

I work in a GP practice and was asked to see a woman who had been a victim of domestic violence. I did see her and thought I had helped her a little, but she stopped coming to see me after about six sessions. It was therefore a shock to receive a letter from a solicitor six months later asking for my notes on this client, who had decided to prosecute her husband. I felt really set up and very worried as the notes I had made, which were few, were not as she might have imagined about her wicked husband, but about her reaction to the way she experienced him as treating her.

We now live in a much more litigious society than we have ever done, and it is wise to take account of this when we are writing our notes. If a client asks you for her notes, you are expected to supply them, and if a court subpoenas you, you must comply and appear with your notes if that is what is asked for.

I was seeing a woman who had been referred to me from the organization that she worked for. She had suffered an accident in the workplace and I was treating her for post-traumatic stress, but I

> also had in mind her dysfunctional family. I felt that her difficulty of coming to terms with the accident was related to a very unhappy background, but I hadn't begun to think with my client about this aspect of her problem, it was too soon. When she decided to sue the organization and asked me for her notes it put me in a terrible dilemma. My notes had not been meant for anybody to see except my supervisor.

It is difficult to explain our way of thinking to anyone who does not know our business, and particularly hard to let our clients see our notes which, although commonplace to us, might appear alarming to them. So what should we do?

A lot of thought was given to this dilemma when the Data Protection Act was introduced in 1984 and the Access to Personal Files Act in 1987. Practitioners who were working in institutions were advised not to keep official notes with names, addresses and identifying features on them. Many therapists now deal with the problem by writing two sets of notes, one to be seen by someone who is not a therapist and another set for themselves. This might seem to be rather a lot of note writing, but they need only be brief, unless you have a particular desire to remember something in detail, or if you are taking the notes to supervision.

Whether you write your notes on a computer or by hand, it is crucial that the names of your clients do not appear. Have two separate systems, one for billing that includes names, addresses and practical details and another for your client's notes, separately identified by a number. A simple system is to keep your clients' notes in a file, not identifiable, which can be easily available when you see your clients. You can then jot a few points down between sessions.

By law you must keep business records for seven years. You do not need to keep clinical files for that long, but if a client returns after many years' absence, it can be a great relief to find that you still have the notes.

I like to keep a record of all the clients I have seen, for no particular reason other than it is, along with my diaries, a record of all the work I have done.

Confidentiality

If you are asked to write a paper you will want to draw on your clinical experience, but you need to be very careful to disguise completely any cases where clients might be identified. If the paper is to be published and there is the slightest chance of a client being able to recognize himself, you must show him the paper and ask for his permission to use his case. This is, of course, a terribly sensitive area and one that only you can judge at the time, but unless the validity of the paper hangs on one client's particular case, discretion might be the better part of valour. You could use a composite of clients when writing for lectures or publication.

Professional wills

Some years ago a colleague and I had to cope with the sudden serious illness and subsequent death of another colleague whose list of patients we both held. She lived alone, but had given her daughter our names in the event of anything happening to her. As it happens, the therapist was able to telephone me before going into hospital. My colleague and I shared out the list and telephoned the patients to let them know that their therapist was unwell and would not be working for some time. (We could not risk the delay in writing a letter.) We said we would get in touch again once the situation was clearer. We each gave our name and telephone number and stressed that we were professional colleagues. When the therapist died we each spoke to the same patients we had contacted earlier in order to tell them. We offered to see anyone who wanted to talk in person, though only two took up this offer. One wanted help to find another therapist, and the other needed two individual sessions in order to express her distress. I have heard of situations where a family member of a deceased therapist has contacted patients and all sorts of boundary complications have ensued, such as patients being invited to become friends of the family and given information which was inappropriate, while colleagues who should have been told were kept in the dark.

It is now commonplace for professional bodies to demand that you make a professional will. To ensure that your clients will be notified and taken care of in the event of your incapacity or death, it is a very good idea to put a will in place, even if you are not required to do so. None of us is immortal and it is good to have contingency plans in place, in case you might suddenly be struck down.

You will need to ask two close colleagues – it is helpful if they know each other – to hold a list of your clients. The list should contain your present clients' names, telephone numbers, email addresses and postal addresses and the day and time of their sessions. Send both your colleagues the list and let each one know who their fellow holder is and how to get in touch with them. The list should be in a sealed envelope to preserve anonymity and only opened if needed. You must also let someone close to you have your colleagues' names and telephone numbers, so that in the event of your sudden demise they can set the ball rolling. You will need to remind yourself to keep the list up to date.

Insurance

You will need to have two sorts of insurance: third party insurance in case your client slips on your hall floor, concusses himself and makes a claim for damages, and professional indemnity insurance in case someone decides to sue you for malpractice. To have them both in place is mandatory, and will also give you peace of mind.

It is possible to have third party insurance attached to your domestic policy, but you must declare that a certain number of clients visit you each week, which might increase the premium. You might prefer to take out a policy especially for your business; the separation of home from business makes tax relief simpler to manage and means the renewal notices will come straight to you.

There are many insurance companies that offer professional indemnity and specialize in insuring psychotherapists, psychoanalysts and counsellors. Ask around for recommendations and choose one that has been in existence for many years.

If clients are insured with BUPA or another private medical insurance company they may be entitled to receive therapy under their policy. Most companies require you to be registered with them before they agree to fund a case. A simple telephone call to their office enables you to find out whether you are eligible to be a registered practitioner with them. If you are eligible and your clients wish their insurers to pay the therapy bills, you will need to agree a method of payment with your clients.

Quite a few of my clients have private health insurance and they are often able to claim for some therapy sessions on their policies. I have made sure that I am a registered practitioner with a number of insurance companies. When I give my clients the invoice I say that my contract is with them, not the insurance company, and therefore do not want to wait until the claim has been processed to be paid. No one has ever queried this arrangement.

It is a good idea to let your clients know how you would like your invoice to be paid while you are arranging to see them through a private health scheme.

Income tax

If you are self-employed, you are required by law to fill in a tax return form, so there is no escape even if your earnings fall below the threshold for paying tax. Unless you are particularly adept with figures and happy to wrestle with the complexities of HM Revenue and Customs guidelines, I suggest you find yourself an accountant. If you can set up a system that you understand right at the start of your therapeutic career and do it with an accountant you trust, it will save you a lot of stress and panic when your year end rolls inexorably around and you have to submit your accounts.

It will also save a lot of panic if you have kept all your receipts and have a record of your business expenses, which will include: telephone calls, stationery, professional conferences, business journeys and any other expenses you have incurred during the course of the year. You will need to work out the percentage of domestic heating and lighting that you have used, and register any expenses you have incurred for the cleaning of your consulting room. A good accountant will help you to think all this through and enable you to get maximum tax relief for your expenses. Remember, you need to keep all your financial records for seven years – it is the law.

You do not have to think about paying VAT unless you are expecting to earn over £73,000 (2012) per year, and then you should take advice about whether you need to charge VAT to your clients. Some medical professions are VAT-exempt and it is a grey area. Taxation can be a grey area both practically and metaphorically speaking.

Your home as your business

Working from home is ubiquitous in the UK and there is no legislation to prevent you doing so. With the advance in telecommunications in the 1980s it became increasingly possible for people to work from home, and teleworking is now enjoyed by millions of people. There have been some attempts to levy business taxes when part of the home has been deemed to be an office, but they have failed. I do not know of any legal or commercial reason why you should not set up your practice at home, but it is wise to check this out with your lawyer or accountant.

It is sensible to be aware of any impact that your business might have on those close by; if you work in a flat you need to make sure that your neighbours are not disturbed by the coming and goings of your clients, and, if parking is a problem in your neighbourhood, it is best if your clients are not seen to be occupying precious parking places. You will want to ensure that any party walls are soundproof and that any communal passageways are clear for your clients and neighbours alike.

I have moved house many times during my career. I have worked at home with small children needing to be taken care of while I saw my clients, I built a consulting room in the garden of one house, I have rented rooms in communal buildings and worked from a flat in one city while living in another. From time to time my resourcefulness has been tested to the limit, particularly when I lived and worked in different cities, but I have never experienced the stress that the following move engendered. We had chosen a large flat in central London, which was beautiful and had all the facilities we needed; crucially, it included a basement where I could see clients. Finally, after weeks of renovating we moved in and I was able to work again. Within a week I had received a most abusive letter from two sets of neighbours saying that I could not see what they considered to be 'mad people' in the building. This was followed closely by a letter from the council saying that I had to pay business rates for the flat. I was beside myself; I saw my whole career at risk. The stress was appalling, but I took advice from professionals and had some judicious conversations with the other neighbours and all was resolved. I did not have to pay the council business rates; it was noted that half of Parliament worked from their homes in my area; as for the neighbours who had complained and had, I imagine, mischievously alerted the council, they left the building.

Continuing professional development (CPD)

Most of the therapeutic professions expect their members to achieve a certain number of hours each year that count towards CPD. It is helpful, and will save you a lot of time at the end of the year, if you record the activities that will contribute to your CPD hours. It is simple to keep a note of the study days and conferences you attend; most of these will provide proof of attendance. It is easy to record the hours of supervision and other professional activities as they occur; just as with tax issues, a daily record is all it needs to keep our systems straight and up to date.

Ethical issues

> The purpose of a Code of Ethics is to define general principles and to establish standards of professional conduct for psychotherapists in their work and to inform and protect those members of the public who seek their services. (United Kingdom Council for Psychotherapy UKCP)

Clients have a right to expect that we act in an ethical manner, by which I mean that they must be able to trust that we are acting in their best interests. It is often difficult for clients who have, for example, grown up within a family whose currency is emotional blackmail, who have never had their feelings taken seriously, or have been psychologically or physically abused, to believe that we have a benign interest in them and that we want to understand their problems rather than sit in judgement of them.

Underpinning all our work is a basic belief and understanding that we will not retaliate, collapse or withdraw our availability to our clients however difficult or unpleasant a session is. That is why we aim, as far as we possibly can, to maintain a continuity of work and offer a thoughtful and thought-through response to whatever experience our clients bring.

All organizations and professional societies will have a code of ethics and a code of conduct for you to refer to. However, no formal code of ethics or conduct can substitute for your own integrity. It is implicit in the unwritten contract we have with our clients that, to the very best of our ability, we will be available at the times agreed upon, that we will not suddenly and without very good reason change an appointment, that we will maintain complete confidentiality, that we will not burden our clients with our own problems and that we will never in any way abuse the powerful position we hold.

Seeing children who bring material to their sessions which raises concerns about their safety at home is, of course, extremely troubling. At the start of treatment I am always careful to let children and parents know the boundaries of confidentiality in my work with them. If I feel a child is in a worrying situation, I will always talk to them about speaking to their parents and the other grown-ups if necessary. And then I speak with the parents. It is always very difficult, but it is always the right thing to do.

How we organize and conduct our practice is a reflection of who we are. The ethical waters within which we swim will be apparent to our clients by our conduct and the way we run our practice. By being dependable, reliable and straightforward we are letting them know where we locate ourselves in the business of therapy; if they feel it is a safe and containing place, they will be able to make best use of the therapy we have to offer them.

I am a couple therapist and only see couples together as a rule, but I had agreed to see a man on his own when his wife refused to come with him. Quite soon divorce proceedings were set in motion and it became apparent that my client wanted me to appear in court, or at least write a letter to the effect that I had invited his wife, more than once, to attend the sessions. I got very nervous about my potential role in this case and turned to the Chair of my Ethics Committee for advice. They were very helpful and I felt completely supported by them.

It is useful to remind ourselves that ethics committees are there for therapists and clients alike.

Data protection

I had been to a case discussion in London and taken my diary and notes with me. We had worked hard all day and went for a meal afterwards. I remember coming out of the restaurant and think I put my briefcase on top of the car while I unlocked the door; it was pouring with rain and I got into the car as quickly as I could. I drove off and I guess the briefcase fell off immediately. I telephoned the restaurant as soon as I realized what had happened; miraculously it had been found and handed in to them. Such was my anxiety I paid for a courier to bring the case to my home that same evening.

This is a nightmare that we would hope never to experience. Under the Data Protection Act we are responsible for protecting all sensitive and personal information that we are privy to and must take great care to keep our clients' records private and safe.

Emails

Emails also fall under the Data Protection Act. Clients now use emails to communicate with us as a matter of course. It is often more efficient to respond to an email than to a voicemail. There may then, however, be a trail of email messages from clients on your computer; it is wise to delete them, especially if you have a laptop that you carry around with you. Leaving your laptop on a bus or train does not bear thinking about.

Writing to clients by email has become commonplace over the past few years, but I would always keep messages short and clear. In fact any communications with clients outside the consulting room should be kept brief. It is best not to enter into a dialogue or allow yourself to be pushed into giving advice. All information needs to be brought to the sessions to be worked on, and you do not want to leave a trail of messages that could lead to misunderstandings or accusations. Like all situations that require such attention to detail and caution, it can seem as if you are being excessive, even paranoid, but should you be put to the test it will show that you have been very sensible indeed.

The paper trail

Through the work we do for our professional bodies and societies we can generate a great deal of paper such as minutes of meetings, drafts of new legislation, membership lists and plans for study days. None of this is very sensitive material and we often allow it to accumulate, believing that one day it might be useful.

My diminutive friend and colleague was characterized by the oversized bag she had carried for years; in fact she never appeared without it until one day her back went and she had to resort to a pull-along shopping basket. She needed such a large bag because she recorded in longhand every meeting, conference and committee that she attended and, as she was the most conscientious and hardworking of people, that was a great many. It is true to say that she was gently mocked for her excessive note taking; she would agree that it was a neurosis and add that she was incapable of listening unless she wrote at the same time. However, my friend's neurosis was regarded as a talent when we were asked to catalogue, for our society, details of its history. We spent hours trawling through her filing system, which was the size of a small government department. My friend had thrown nothing away for over 30 years and we managed to compile the most wonderful and detailed archive for posterity.

It can be rewarding to be able to find material for an archive, but you need to weigh up the benefit of hoarding old papers against the disadvantage of a cluttered room. It can be pleasurable to settle to the task of deciding what you want to keep and what you want to discard.

Much miscellaneous information, such as newsletters, leaflets and pamphlets, can be thrown away, but you might want to keep professional journals and publications. If you have room to store them it is pleasing to include them in your library of professional books. They are useful to refer to and can be a resource for your colleagues too.

Lending books, particularly to trainees and supervisees, can be a problem so it is important to have your name in the book and to keep a list of who has got what. I have only lost one important book in over thirty years; I always enjoy contacting a colleague and saying that so many years ago on such and such a date, they borrowed a certain book and now I would like it back! It is never stolen . . . just forgotten.

A question of time

Self-employed people in general, and therapists in particular, fail to put a value on the time they spend on paperwork and all the other demands that accompany a professional working life. If you ask a therapist how much work they do they will tell you about the face-to-face client hours, but might completely discount time spent in supervision, writing notes, preparing the invoices, tracking payments, writing letters to GPs and other professionals, sorting out insurance, responding to enquiries, keeping abreast of the professional literature, attending CPD events, supporting their society, being members of committees, setting up sessions, cleaning the consulting room and tidying the hallways.

Yet all these activities contribute to our clients experience of us, and are part of the business of therapy.

5

Boundaries

The main street door of the apartments had not closed properly, and an opportunistic robber climbed the stairs with a crowbar and started to break open the front door of my flat while I was seeing a client. I went to it and exclaimed (through the closed door) 'Stop that at once', or words to that effect, and returned to my client to the sounds of my would-be intruder's retreating footsteps. Well, what else could one do?

This unusual, but nevertheless true, event serves to illustrate our commitment as therapists to keep our clients safe. It is part of our unwritten contract that, to the best of our ability, we will protect the therapeutic space from intrusions of any kind. This therapist was fearless in her determination to do just that; the boundary she was protecting between herself with her client and the outside world was both physical and psychological. Like a mother with her baby, all thoughts of her own safety were abandoned to the need to protect her vulnerable charge.

In the previous chapters we have looked at the importance of the practical aspects of setting up a practice, from the voicemail message to the billing system, from soundproof rooms to tax returns. By paying attention to such details, which might be considered superfluous to the business of therapy, we create a safe and containing environment within which we can do our work. It is unlikely that our potential clients will consciously judge us by our voicemail message, but every piece of information they have about us, both conscious and unconscious, will be used to inform their decision about whether or not to choose us as their therapist.

However, therapy is an extraordinary business and therapists know that it is as important to pay attention to the psychological environment as it is to consider the physical environment within which our work is conducted. This is particularly so when we are considering the boundaries around the therapeutic space – boundaries which extend beyond the consulting room itself.

All professionals regard the work they do with their clients as confidential. None of us would expect our professional adviser to reveal the information we have given to them to the outside world: the lawyer would not divulge the nature of their clients' business and our doctor must respect our privacy and not reveal details of our ailments. The therapeutic relationship demands more than that. The need for discretion extends beyond the consulting room or office; it is the therapeutic relationship itself that must remain confidential unless the client himself chooses to reveal its existence.

Protecting the client/therapist boundary

I had planned the move into our new house so carefully. The builders were going to leave in July and I was going to resume my work in September; plenty of time to get settled, or so I thought. We moved in, but the builders hadn't finished and as September approached it became apparent that I would have to see my clients while the builders were still in situ. It was hell on earth. The noise of the drilling and hammering went on all day, and from time to time the front door was left open as workmen came and went. The effort of maintaining a protected space for my client was enormous — like a mother who was trying to keep her newborn baby asleep. I experienced all the outside activity as a disturbing threat and potentially destructive to the relationship between me and my client.

Sometimes even the best-laid plans go awry and we have to deal
with difficult situations as they arise. I find it best, when something
beyond my control threatens to impinge on the work, to tackle
it head on. A client was about to leave when I heard voices just
outside the consulting room door; I realized that a delivery had
arrived and was being signed for, so I told my client I would go
into the hall 'to make sure it is safe for you to leave'.

When the peace of my consulting room was shattered by
a terrible screeching noise, which turned out to be the central
heating pump, I decided it was best to leave the room and deal
with the problem rather than suffer in non-silence.

Neighbours

I live in a quiet suburban street, and from time to time one neighbour
or another will remark upon clients who they have noticed as they
go to and from my house. They never ask me who they are, but
occasionally, when curiosity gets the better of them, they will draw

my attention to a client who might have left my house in tears, or spent minutes on the telephone outside their house complaining about something, or someone! I was once told that a strange man sat on my doorstep for a good half hour after he left the session; occasionally a neighbour will think they have recognized a client and I am obliquely asked for confirmation that they are right.

A therapist would have to be made of stone not to be interested in what their clients get up to after they close their front door, but if the therapeutic boundary is to be upheld we must respect our clients' privacy once their session is over. You need to gain an understanding of your clients from the work you do in the sessions, from the material they bring to you and not from someone else's observations – no matter how intriguing these might be. But you must also respect your neighbours' healthy curiosity about what is going on in their street; they will not necessarily understand how crucial it is for you keep your professional boundary absolutely watertight. So do not pull yourself up to your full professional height and say self-righteously, 'I never talk about my clients'; all you need to do is smile and nod and change the subject. Most of your neighbours will quickly get the point.

The same applies to supper parties or any social gathering; you do not want to be regarded as a gossipy therapist, so it is best not to talk about any clients no matter how anonymous you make them. If one of your clients is mentioned during the course of a conversation try to mentally disengage; this can be particularly difficult if you are seeing a well-known personality. To maintain complete confidentiality, and not bask in reflected glory, is a sacrifice we must make; what makes it worse is that no one knows just how noble we are being!

The boundary between you and your client

Within the consulting room the boundary between you and your client is all-important and much of the work that you do will no doubt reflect this. The nature of therapy requires your boundary to be permeable, and from time to time you may want to reflect on the way your client experiences his closeness to you. You may want to explore in the transference, within the relationship with you, the flexibility of boundaries that is required in order to have an intimate relationship. This is particularly the case if you are working with a couple. As my supervisor put it, 'The emotional gate needs to be able to swing to and fro – it should never be stuck in one position, either wide open or tight shut.'

All the conditions we put in place enable us to be open and available to our clients in a way that would be impossible in any other situation. It is the firmness of the boundary of time, place and professionalism that allows the boundaries between client and therapist to be permeable and flexible. The therapist can be hated and loved; rejected and accepted; the client can safely experience intimacy with an other – you.

If we are to preserve this unique working environment it is inadvisable to have a relationship with our clients outside the consulting room. If a client asks what they should do if they bump into you outside the sessions, you can explore the dilemma with him, but usually an unspoken protocol will exist which both client and therapists instinctively adhere to, each recognizing and acknowledging the distinct nature of their relationship. If they meet in the street or at the cinema they might nod in each other's direction, but then pass quickly by. I would never approach a client and I always leave it up to him to decide whether he is going to acknowledge me or not.

My husband and I had been invited to a charity event. I was really enjoying myself and having an animated conversation with someone who I had not seen for years, when I spotted, out of the corner of my eye, a client who I had seen very recently for a couple of consultations. I kept him in the periphery of my vision and carried on talking to my friend intending to keep well away from him, which would not be difficult as we were in a large room and there were many people present. However, he clearly had a different idea. Within seconds of my noticing him he was by my side saying how nice it was to see me, and asking me how long I had been involved in the charity. I answered him as briefly as possible and moved away, but he followed and sat next to me during the speeches, telling me who each speaker was and how he had come to know many of them. I was utterly miserable; I could not move and felt completely intruded upon. Later, at the reception, he insisted on introducing me to his wife. I decided discretion was the better part of valour and left the party early.

You might think this therapist was being unduly sensitive and perhaps a little precious. Why should it matter so much that she was being manoeuvred into a social relationship with this client? After all, she had only seen him twice. If she had been his lawyer they would have had a perfectly reasonable conversation and their working relationship would not be compromised.

It matters because a therapist is giving her client more than just her professional expertise; she is offering him, for a limited and prescribed period of time, her whole self and attention, which comes without judgement or criticism, thus allowing her client to explore and discover aspects of himself and his relationships with others that he might never before have acknowledged, either to himself or to anyone else. This is a difficult and challenging business and only made possible by putting in place the intimacy of anonymity — a paradox that requires hard work and discipline to achieve and maintain.

I have heard of therapists who offer their clients a cup of tea when they arrive. This is not in itself bad practice and I am sure it feels comforting when you arrive at your therapist's door on a cold and wet afternoon, but it might make it difficult to display the more disagreeable and hostile parts of yourself to such a kindly person! However . . .

My therapist always made me a cup of tea when I arrived for my session. He was very clear about his boundaries and I would say a very orthodox therapist, but the fact that he made me a cup of tea was comforting and I found myself able to talk to him about things that I had never told anyone else. So when I became a therapist I found no difficulty in offering a distressed client a cup of tea. I find that for some clients in some situations it is helpful – it doesn't compromise the therapeutic relationship at all.

This anecdote illustrates the influence our own therapy has on the way we work, and highlights the fact that theoretical boundaries can sometimes be flexible too.

The boundary of time

I really liked my client; she was a sensitive and responsive soul and psychologically minded. She readily explored her past and responded appropriately to transference interpretations and would often express her appreciation of the work we were doing. From the beginning of her therapy this client was always a minute or two early and she would never voluntarily notice that her time was up. At first it was like an itch that I would occasionally scratch in an absent-minded way. She was early by such a tiny amount that I thought my clock might be wrong. It was irritating, but in a vague sort of way; after all what difference does a couple of minutes make. However, as time wore on I became annoyed about her early arrival and cross about my difficulty in ending the sessions.

The itch became all-engrossing and I became increasingly aware that this difficulty with time must play an important part in my client's psyche. Eventually I found a way of addressing the seemingly insignificant stolen two minutes. My client knew exactly what I was talking about. 'I always thought this notion of the strict fifty-minute hour was ridiculous,' she said. 'Why should you have all the control?' At this point I knew that we had started the beginning of the ending of my client's therapy: we had managed to address the elephant in the room.

Whether it is the 50-minute hour or the 60-minute hour, it is an essential fact of therapeutic life that the timing of a session is strictly adhered to. Clients often get extremely frustrated by our determination to stick to our guns, but it is important that we do so. How our clients use or abuse their allocated time with us can tell us so much about them. The story above shows us that the extra two minutes, which would go completely unnoticed in the outside world, can be of great help to an observant therapist; in this case it was recognized as a bid for autonomy and a challenge to authority. In the microscopic world of the consulting room a minute can speak volumes.

> It was usually such a struggle to get her to leave and for me not to lose a sense of time in the counter-transference. It was so much easier to think about when I was not with her . . . I guess what I do far more now is to bring it to her attention; recognize her anger and difficulty in leaving and say, 'What is happening here?' Put simply, I see the infringements of boundaries as testing the relationship between us.

The therapeutic hour can seem interminable; sometimes it feels as if the clock has stopped and I pray for a session to end, but it can equally feel as if no time at all has passed when it is time to finish. Our perception of time helps to inform us about the unconscious as well as conscious process that is taking place in our consulting room, and as such is grist to our therapeutic mill.

How we structure our time between clients, though a pragmatic business, is nevertheless worth paying attention to. It is good to allow yourself enough time between clients to write a few notes, make yourself a cup of tea or use the telephone. Many therapists, while paying strict attention to the therapeutic boundaries with their clients, find it difficult to take their own need for a boundary seriously. We too need to put a structure in place that gives us time and space to process the work we are doing.

Many therapists like to have a predictable schedule and only see clients on the hour; others find themselves working to a more fluid structure which bends to the needs of their clients. I know of one therapist who felt a seismic change for the better when she decided to have a 20-minute break between sessions. Looking after yourself is as important as looking after your clients.

The question of gifts and artefacts

This is difficult territory. Attitudes towards receiving presents vary enormously. Some therapists would not accept a gift under any circumstances, while others find it hard to refuse a small offering

of appreciation. You may choose to put up a very firm boundary which says 'no' to presents; however, if you have not got such a clear policy, each situation will present you with not only a challenge, but also an opportunity to think with your client, perhaps not immediately, but at a later date, about the meaning of his gesture.

Clients may also bring objects to their sessions such as photographs, letters and other personal items that are important to them. Again, attitudes differ about how much notice to take of such concrete representations of a client's world, but if the therapeutic container is clearly in place it should be possible to incorporate such objects into your work with the client and think not only about the meaning of the object but also about the reason for bringing it.

It is painful to recall, but I remember, as a newly qualified couple therapist, completely ignoring a notice that the wife brought to a session. I had a sofa in my consulting room and as this couple sat down she placed a card between the two of them, I think it said something like 'I hate him'; I blush when I think of it now, but I didn't refer to the notice during the whole of their session. In spite of this rather odd episode they stayed with me for some time, but they never referred to it and neither did I.

Who among us has not at one time or another wished that we could go back and do the session again?

Crossing the boundaries

The mobile telephone is now ubiquitous and many sessions are interrupted by its demanding ring. The ring can be anything from a full orchestral rendition of 'Land of Hope and Glory' to the sound of a baby's cry; whatever it is, it penetrates the therapeutic boundary and insists that it is paid attention to. The reasons for the phone being left switched on will be as diverse as the callers, and it is for the therapist to decide how best to address its presence. You might issue a warning as they do at the theatre that 'all mobile phones must be switched off', or you might decide to tackle each interruption as it arises. The point is to recognize that it is a breach of the boundaries, a point that can easily be overlooked as we are all so used to its demanding place in our lives. I write this rather shamefacedly as I realize how often I have swallowed my irritation and not challenged the interruption.

Bottles of water and takeaway cups of coffee can also be a source of irritation when clients arrive clutching them in their hands. I may be asked if I object, and sometimes I do, but I find it surprisingly difficult to say so. However, these small breaches of our boundaries, if recognized, understood and spoken to can often move the work on. Stretching across the boundary between the outside world and the inside world of the therapeutic space you can, in that unguarded moment, catch an unauthorized glimpse of your client's inner world.

Extending the therapeutic space

I was asked by a social worker if I would see someone who was completely incapacitated; this woman was living in a nursing home and could not possibly travel to a therapist, but she was very troubled and needed to speak to a counsellor. I talked to my supervisor about the request, as I felt anxious on several counts. How, I wondered, could I create a therapeutic container outside my usual physical and psychological space; how could privacy and confidentiality be protected, and would I be able to cope with someone as disabled as this client appeared to be?

After much deliberation I decided that I would at least have an initial consultation with this person and see if it would be possible to work with her. Twelve months later I am still visiting my client once a week. I am very clear about the time that I visit, which is the same each week, and closely guard the confidentiality of the sessions from well-meaning relatives who, because of the circumstances, know that I am visiting and want to offer me their opinions and views on my client's problems.

As well as dealing with well-meaning friends and relatives I also encounter other difficulties that I do not experience when I am working with clients at home. I never know whether my client will be sitting in a chair or lying in bed when I arrive and I do not know whether she will be able to sustain a full fifty-minute session or not. The work we do is informed as much by her physical situation as by her emotional and mental state, and within the allocated time I am as accommodating and flexible as possible; I sometimes just sit quietly by her side. We have done some remarkable work and I am very pleased that I accepted the challenge.

It is of course for you to decide if you want to work outside your usual parameters. It is unusual for a client to ask for on-going therapy within a hospital setting. Social workers would not adhere to the same therapeutic boundaries as the therapist who tells this story – indeed, they could not possibly fulfil their caseload if they did. Should such a case be presented to you, it is worth considering. Maintaining boundaries in order to accommodate a client who cannot come to you is an interest-ing exercise. 'If the mountain will not come to Mohammed, Mohammed must go to the mountain', but the boundaries must also go with him.

However, if you are asked to see a celebrity outside your con-sulting room it may be a different matter. Bear in mind that even King George VI went at first to his speech therapist's consulting room, as did Princess Diana while seeing her psychotherapist.

Hospital visiting is different, and if a client is very sick and asks to see us we can visit briefly without compromising any future work we might do. A therapist who had been seeing her client for many years, willingly visited him at home when he was terminally ill. Some extreme situations require a response that might be a breach of our usual boundaries and demand flexibility from the therapist.

Telephone calls, emails and letters

As I have said before, it is always better to keep any communication outside the consulting room as brief as possible. Unless you work part time and are rarely at home, or have peripatetic clients, there is little to be gained from your client being able to reach you on your mobile phone. The text message, while quick and easy, pays scant attention to the subtle boundaries that we are working so hard to maintain, and the quickness and ease of communication that they offer is at odds with the thoughtful response that we want to give to our clients.

Emails can also, if we let them, allow for too casual a communication, but they are very convenient and can avoid our playing telephone tag with our clients. They are useful when an appointment needs to be changed or cancelled, but not if they are being used as a way of extending the sessions. The ease and speed with which we are able to respond to a message can mean that we say too much too quickly, and without enough thought. We do not want to put anything in writing that can be misunderstood or taken out of context.

> It is a good discipline to apply the principles of letter writing to emails – something I encourage in my colleagues – indeed some might say I nag them.

Letters take longer to write, and in the process of writing them we spend time thinking about our turn of phrase; we are aware that the tone of the letter will matter to the reader and take care to ensure that there will be no misunderstandings. There is a profound difference between writing a letter and an email; the email is immediate dialogue and, as such, the communication can be casual and suggest a false intimacy. A letter upholds the boundaries. This more formal method of communication reflects the fact that the unique and intimate relationship between client and therapist only happens within the confines of the consulting room.

Telephone sessions

There might be occasions when it seems appropriate and helpful to offer your client a session on the telephone. I have done it once or twice and find it very hard work. Information is transmitted in countless ways other than the spoken word, and the silence which is such an important part of communication is hard to maintain when you are on the telephone. If you do agree to work this way it is important to set the boundary of time and make sure that you are both clear about what you are offering, why it is being offered and how it will be paid for. The client should bear the cost of the call and therefore be the one to call in; so agree beforehand, either by email or in a session, the time that he will call. Be ready by the telephone.

The crisis telephone call

My client telephoned me in desperation. He said he felt out of control and wanted to kill either himself or his wife; what could he do? His wife had been harassing him all morning and she knew that he was on a very short fuse. I felt alarmed, and knew that this couple could create terrible tensions between themselves and that he could lose his temper in a potentially violent way. But I also knew, because I had been seeing them for a couple of years, that my client was a deeply caring person and that he would not have telephoned me if he had not wanted to manage the way he was feeling.

He did not want to act out his fury. I kept calm and suggested he went for a walk around the local park, which had featured in some of the sessions as a safe haven. I also offered to see both him and his wife for an extra session.

This therapist had to think on her feet and keep her nerve. She was responsive to her client, but did not encourage a lengthy dialogue on the telephone, which would have been inappropriate, particularly as her client was the couple, not just him. She contained his anxiety by remaining calm and by suggesting that he went for a walk in the park – a reminder of the work they had done together, and that she could hold him in mind. She then confirmed that the work was with the couple by offering them a joint extra session. The telephone call was kept short, the client was contained and further help was offered, but in the consulting room. The call was sensitively responded to without breaking the boundaries.

It is worth remembering that no electronic communications can be guaranteed to be secure and confidential.

Couple work

Nowhere are boundaries more in evidence than when you are working with a couple. In a joint session the Oedipal configuration is clear for all to see, and during the course of a session the couple can be experienced in several different ways. One of the clients may imagine that he and the therapist are forming an alliance or that his partner and the therapist are the couple. Many imaginary pairings are possible, but when such fantasies take place and they are contained within the consulting room, helpful interpretations can be made that illuminate the clients' Oedipal dilemmas.

I work with a co-therapist, which can be extremely helpful when seeing couples, but it requires my co-therapist and me to be adept at managing our own boundaries. Over the past 20 years or so that we have worked together, we have developed subtle but clear boundaries. We have an unspoken agreement that, while allowing ourselves a particular intimacy within the confines of the consulting room, we do not socialize or enquire too deeply into one another's private lives. If either of us is going through a difficult time we will be concerned and as helpful as possible, but we do not assume that we must know all that is happening or that we have a right to pursue the matter.

The enduring couple is the client couple. Even if they are in the deepest of conflicts they are still a couple. When they leave the consulting room they carry on with a relationship, either loving or hateful, from which the couple therapist is excluded, and it is the therapist who has to manage her own Oedipal feelings of being left out. The boundary is clear; once the couple leave the consulting room they have an opportunity to discuss their session and their feelings about it with complete disregard for the therapist. This brings sharply into focus a feature of all the work that we do: we are not, nor should we be, the most important person in our clients' lives.

The therapist's boundaries

We have all heard stories of practitioners who have abused the unique and trusting relationship that exists between a therapist and her client. To take sexual advantage of someone who is vulnerable and dependent on us is of course outrageous and should never happen. There are very serious consequences if it does occur. To use, for our own benefit, information we might gain during the course of the work with our client is obviously immoral, and using any clinical material in publications without gaining permission from our clients is a breach of confidentiality. There is a case for considering disclosing dangerous criminal behaviour to the authorities. All of this and more is clearly spelt out in the code of ethics and conduct of the professional bodies and there will be a complaints procedure for your clients to follow should they need to.

But what of the more subtle breaches of our professional boundaries that only we are privy to?

The dependent therapist

I had many years of therapy, and felt it was time to finish. Every time I tried to talk to my therapist about leaving she would make an interpretation to the effect that I was angry with her, or not allowing myself to look at something, or afraid of being attached to her. It was impossible. In the end I just stopped going to see her.

There is sometimes a fine line between letting a client go too soon, and holding on to a client for too long. There may be many reasons why it might be inconvenient for a client to leave us; as one therapist thought wistfully to herself when her client told her that he wanted to finish, 'But what about my new stair carpet?' It is a good therapist who can allow herself to recognize such ignoble thoughts, while she gets on with the business of therapy and helps her client to work towards a satisfactory ending.

Interest, curiosity or nosiness

To be interested in our clients is inherent in the work that we do; in fact if we were not interested in the human condition in general, and our clients in particular, we could not do our job. We are curious to find out why our clients find themselves in the predicaments they do, and interested to understand what has brought them to therapy. But we often have to persuade our clients to join with us and be curious about their own lives. Many people, when initially asked about their childhood, shrug and say something like, 'Well, it was normal'; as if to ask 'What is there to think about?' It is a sign that therapy is truly under way when your client realizes that you are genuinely interested in who they really are.

There is, however, a difference between being curious and being nosy. Your interest needs to follow your client for his sake rather than for your own satisfaction. It can be frustrating when a client has agonized about something in a session and then does not mention it again. How and if you pursue the matter is a subtle business. If you are simply interested because you want the satisfaction of knowing what the outcome has been, your client will quite rightly smell a nosy rat. It is the suspension of personal curiosity and because we have no investment in the answer that our clients can trust that we are genuinely interested in them.

Self-promotion

My therapist was an artist and there would often be signs of her work in progress in her entrance hall and consulting room. It was an aspect of her that I rather liked; I enjoyed knowing that my therapist had talents and was interested in things other than therapy. But my feelings towards her changed when she gave me an invitation to her art show. I don't really understand why, but I felt compelled to go to the exhibition. I resented being asked.

It is always better to resist the temptation to cross the therapeutic boundary. The client who felt compelled to go to the exhibition, but was resentful about being asked, is reflecting the dilemma of crossing boundaries. She was no doubt compelled to go because within the consulting room there would be a special relationship taking place, a transference relationship, within which her therapist might represent a mother or father who had to be obeyed or pleased at all costs. Whatever this particular client's situation was, she recognized, correctly, that the invitation was a step too far.

Invitations

Invitations can be also issued from clients to their therapists, and sometimes it feels very difficult to refuse them, particularly if the invitation comes after the client has left. I was invited to a wedding by a couple who I had seen for a short period of time, specifically to help them sort out their pre-wedding nerves. I liked this couple very much and it seemed appropriate for me to receive the invitation. After a great deal of thought I decided to attend the ceremony but not the reception; I waited outside the church long enough to congratulate the couple, and then slipped away.

This crossing of the boundaries seemed appropriate, but when another couple, who I had been seeing for many years, moved away and invited me to visit them in their new home, there was no possibility of my being able to accept their invitation. We all recognized that the intimate relationship, which had allowed so much work to take place in the consulting room, could never be upheld in the outside world. It had been forged within a safe, predictable and reliable therapeutic space and although it was clearly the case that my clients and I had much in common, it was also the case that towards the end of their time with me I was in receipt of some very positive projections; a transference that would take a long time to dissipate.

From time to time we encounter clients who we can imagine being friends with, and it is a genuine sacrifice to abandon the possibility of forming a friendship; but that is the nature of our very particular and extraordinary business.

Our clients give us permission to know them because of our adherence to the strict therapeutic boundaries. It is our responsibility to uphold them.

6

Support Systems

The fifty minutes were up and my tearful client got up to go. 'It must be so exhausting for you,' she said, tossing the last of many soggy tissues into the waste paper basket. 'I can't imagine how you manage to listen hour after hour and day after day to people moaning and groaning.'

The box of tissues is the tangible evidence that the therapist was prepared for her client's emotional distress, but there are countless ways in which a therapist is prepared for her client which are far less tangible.

The internal capacity of the therapist to contain and ab-

sorb her client's tears, without becoming soggy like the tissues, is developed through her training and maintained by a matrix of resources invisible to her clients, but without which she would not be able to do her job properly.

It is difficult for those unfamiliar with the way we work to understand how this can be so, and when we try to explain it is often thought that our training has rendered us unfeeling, but it is because of the discipline of a professional training and all the structures that we put in place, that it is possible to be empathic without being sentimental, that we can feel our client's emotional state without becoming identified with it, and that we can be wholeheartedly involved in the business of therapy without feeling trapped or overwhelmed.

The capacity to be completely available to our clients while maintaining an emotional distance; to listen to tragic stories without falling into despair; to remain alert and be able to decipher the essential message through the tales of an unhappy life; to encourage the silent client to speak and our verbose client to pause and reflect; to convince our sceptical clients that our interest in them is authentic – all this depends on the quality and resilience of our inner resources and outer support systems.

A professional training

'We were all right until we came to see you,' said my couple accusingly and in unison; 'we weren't terribly happy, but life was bearable; we were able to function. You know – look after the kids, see friends, have some sort of a life. Now it seems as if everything is falling apart: work, family, everything; this therapy is just being destructive.'

It is at times like this (and who among us has not heard such spine-chilling accusations?) that we call upon our training to remind ourselves that we have the credentials to do our work and the professional acumen to carry it through. That does not mean that we should rest on our laurels; we must take our clients' complaints seriously and allow them to express their dissatisfaction with us; we must fasten our seat belts, trusting that the work will continue and that we will all survive.

Although we know from experience and theoretical under-standing that things often get worse before they get better, we can feel dreadful when our clients doubt both us and their therapy. It is at these times that our professional self carries on with the work while we experience the hopelessness that our clients are feeling.

To remain involved while being uninvolved – a participant observer – requires the therapist to occupy a third position, which is acquired first and foremost through her professional training.

Theory

All professional trainings provide a firm theoretical base, which underpins our work and supports us when we feel we have lost our bearings with a client. We should feel contained rather than constricted by theoretical understanding, so that it remains a valuable framework, a reference point from which we can develop our ideas and understanding throughout our careers.

Therapy

Most trainings require their trainees to undergo therapy. It is the lynchpin, and perhaps the most relevant aspect of the training. Whether we are in once-a-week therapy for two years, or five-times-a-week psychoanalysis for ten years, the benefit of encountering oneself in the safety of the consulting room with the help of a psychoanalyst or psychotherapist is of enormous value. The relationship with our therapist, which we eventually internalize, becomes a vital resource for us and will undoubtedly influence the way we work with our clients.

Our therapeutic experience is part of, but separate from, our professional training. As we explore our thoughts and feelings we come to understand a great deal about our unconscious selves. When we take ownership of our less desirable qualities and have the experience of being accepted, warts and all, by our own therapist, we embrace a more accepting and less judgemental part of ourselves; a dimension that we can then make available to our clients. This in turn enables our clients to trust us as they explore the more vulnerable parts of themselves.

Supervision

> The first time I saw my client after my last supervision I was amazed. He walked into my consulting room, sat in the chair, and with a sigh began to speak about his problems in a different way; it was as if he had been party to the conversation my supervisor and I had had about him. I did not need to incorporate the understanding I had gleaned from supervision into the session; my client seemed to have picked it up at an unconscious level.

Your professional organization will require you to have supervision on a regular basis. Good supervision with someone who you respect and who you feel confident with is an invaluable resource. Our work is conducted in such a confidential and private way that to expose it to outside scrutiny is a necessary safeguard. Our supervisors offer us support, constructive criticism and an opportunity to develop our understanding of the work we are doing. Through the reflective prism of supervision we are often able to see aspects of our clients and the work we are doing with them in a different and illuminating light.

Peer group supervision can also be very helpful and rewarding, as it keeps you in touch with colleagues and provides a safe forum in which to explore not only your work but also the more prosaic aspects of running a practice.

Eventually you will also supervise those less experienced than yourself, you might even find yourself supervising the supervisors. It is the nature of the business we do that through our own therapy and supervision we are involved in a self-regulating system which, by its very nature, acknowledges that we are interdependent with one another. In this way we try to make sure that our private practice is good practice.

Returning to our analogy of the set of Russian dolls, you could say that the professional and ethical environment of our particular discipline is the outer doll, which contains the supervisors;

the supervisors contain the therapist, and in turn the therapist contains the client.

Recharging your batteries

It can feel as if we have to work awfully hard to get the support we need. Therapy and supervision do give us inner strength and resources, but they are only as effective as the effort we put into them. It is the effort we put into both that yields such high rewards, the results of which we can draw on daily, but we also need to be nourished in a way that requires less effort from us. Conferences offer us just that opportunity.

You will be bombarded with advertising literature about forthcoming conferences, some local, some abroad, some three-day affairs, some just for the day. The range of subjects is enormous, there is something for everyone; you can choose between subjects that are relevant to the way you work, or attend a seminar just for the sake of interest. Many conferences and seminars will offer a continuing professional development certificate, which will contribute to the number of continuing professional development (CPD) hours that are required by your professional body.

If you belong to a local society or attend meetings of your organization, you will get input for very little cost. If you attend a three-day conference abroad, there will be a significant cost. Although it can often take a major effort to attend such meetings and conferences, it is invariably the case that you will feel replenished and stimulated afterwards, having heard interesting material and no doubt having met friendly colleagues.

Some therapists are very organized, budget for such external events and plan ahead, applying in good time for their preferred conference. Others attend on a haphazard, last-minute basis. Whatever your preferred method, remember that we all need to recharge our batteries from time to time. We can be inspired by a wonderful lecture and come away with renewed vigour feeling that our therapeutic load is a little lighter. Remember also that anything you do that advances your knowledge and capacity to work, be it attending conferences or taking supervision, is tax deductible.

If you are asked to give a lecture or speak at a conference, do seize the opportunity. It can take months of preparation and hard work to write a paper and not infrequently be the cause of great anguish, but to commit yourself to such an endeavour is creative and will build your inner resources and confidence like nothing else does. The rewards can be great.

Professional resources

Your local doctors will not only be a source of referrals, they can also be a source of comfort if you are worried about a client. It is helpful, if you are at all concerned about your client's emotional stability, to ask for his doctor's name at the start of the work. It is then relatively easy to gain permission to speak to your client's doctor if you become concerned for his safety. If your client is in a fragile state and you are to be away for some time, it can be reassuring for both of you to know that the doctor has been alerted to your absence.

It is also good to foster a relationship with a psychiatrist who is sympathetic to the way that you work. If you think that it would be helpful for a client to have a psychiatric assessment, it is useful to be able to suggest a name of someone in whom you have confidence and can trust.

We meet many people in allied professions during the course of our career. If we take the time to respond to any communication from them with courtesy and respect, we will soon build up a support system that from time to time will prove to be an invaluable resource.

My client was very upset. He felt that information was circulating around the town that could only have come from me. Of course the sane part of me knew that this was not so, but such was the paranoia of my client that he almost convinced me I had divulged his secrets.

It is at times like this that you dust off the letter from your professional indemnity insurer. Reliable insurance is a reassuring and crucial part of your support system.

A drink and a peer group

I remember my 18-year-old daughter returning from Canada where she had been au-pairing for a summer job. She had been in an isolated part of the country and her first words to me as she landed at Heathrow were, 'I need a drink and a peer group'.

Being a therapist is a paradoxical business. We can spend all day with people locked in an intimate relationship, which is made possible by the fact that you and your client will part, to all intents and purposes, as strangers at the end of the therapeutic hour. Our work can be a lonely experience, which may become hazardous for both us and our clients if we do not take seriously the extraordinary nature of the business we are in and recognize the need for 'a drink and a peer group'.

> I decided that just because I did not work in an office there was no reason why I should not have a Christmas party with my fellow workers. So I sent an invitation to as many therapists as I could find in my area and invited them to join me in celebrating Christmas with our own office party. The response was overwhelming, and it has become an annual event to look forward to.

This good idea reflects the need we all have for a peer group with whom we can talk shop. We cannot indulge in casual talk about the work we do, and although people might be interested to know just what we get up to in the consulting room, it is very difficult to have a mutually satisfactory conversation about it with someone

who does not understand our business. This of course is not so different from others who work in a specialized field, but we do not have fellow workers who we meet over the water dispenser or for lunch. For the most part we work in fairly isolated conditions.

We have looked at some of the ways that we make contact with our peer group – conferences, seminars, our organization's study days and other events, all of which contribute to us feeling part of a working community. Two therapists joined together to set up a soup kitchen for their colleagues to drop in once a week for lunch. Most networks of therapists have people who will host a reading group. Both of these are really good ways of cementing supportive professional relationships.

Inappropriate support

I saw my analyst for a long time on a regular basis; our work came to a satisfactory end and I did not see her again for years. I returned when life once again became traumatic, thinking that it would be helpful to see someone who already knew me, but this time I had a very different experience. More often than not I found myself listening to my analyst's problems. We often went over time and I think she was more dependent on me than I was on her. I was so fond of my analyst that we continued in this way for a long time; in fact until she became very ill and died.

This sad tale highlights the danger of relying on the relationship we have with our clients for companionship. The boundaries that we looked at in the last chapter can become blurred as we get older. If we find ourselves alone in the world we can imagine that the special and privileged nature of the relationships we have with clients is for real and we forget that we are not part of their lives any more than they are part of ours.

Family and friends

We can underestimate our reliance on family and fail to appreciate how much support we receive from them. When we work at home it can be difficult to leave our clients, metaphorically speaking, in the consulting room, and we may find ourselves inflicting the fallout from a difficult session on whoever happens to be in the house at the time. Occasionally it is very helpful to be able to explode about an impossible client to an understanding spouse and download the accumulated stress of our day with someone we trust, but we need to notice if our nearest and dearest are beginning to wilt under the pressure and find other outlets if our work begins to take precedence over family needs. We can become totally immersed in the all-consuming business of therapy, particularly when we first start our practice, and need to be reminded that there is life outside the consulting room.

My mother was a therapist. She worked at home and when she was seeing clients I had to remain as quiet as possible and keep to the back of the house. I remember spending hours watching the television and waiting for her to finish work. I hated her clients who seemed to get far more attention than I did.

This is a sorry but unfamiliar story. It must be very difficult to have a present but unavailable parent, someone who is willing to listen to the problems of a stranger, but be too busy to hear those of her own child.

Friends can be a valuable part of our support system. Because we do not talk to them about our clients, we are reminded that our work is not the sum total of our parts. Friends help us to put the therapy business into perspective as they offer us a drink and a non-therapy-oriented peer group.

When extra support is necessary

When our personal life is in disarray our container, the support system that we rely on for our daily needs, can come under a great deal of pressure and as a consequence our professional life may feel undermined and vulnerable. We need then to decide how serious the disruption is, how long it might last and think about whether we need to put auxiliary help in place while we ride out the storm.

Situations that affect our working life vary in seriousness; sometimes we do not realize how upset we are and it is up to our friends and colleagues to suggest that we seek professional help. The breakdown of a marriage, a death or serious illness in the family can put us under severe stress; we might need to continue our work because of financial reasons, but find it terribly difficult to do so because of emotional distress. We can find ourselves envying our client's therapy as we wonder who we can ourselves turn to when we need help.

When we encounter such testing circumstances, it is time to turn to our support systems for help. We might decide to take extra supervision or talk to a close colleague; it might be helpful to see a therapist. If we find the strain too much, in spite of extra support, we should consider taking a break. This is a very difficult decision to take, particularly if we are worried about money, but the work is very demanding and although we might be able to coast within our own comfort zone with some clients, it might be impossible to do that for any extended period of time with more demanding cases.

> My daughter called from Spain in a terrible state. Through her uncontrollable sobs she told me that she thought she couldn't carry on any longer. This was at 7.45 in the morning. At 8 o'clock I had to see my first client, so I handed the telephone to my husband and went to my consulting room. Imagine my horror when my client told me that she had just heard that her son, who I knew was only a few months older than my daughter, was having a psychotic breakdown while on his gap year in Paris. It was an agonizing 50 minutes.

This therapist was of course relying on her husband to contain their daughter on the telephone while she contained her client. In this case she had to call on all her inner resources to enable her to continue to work with her client's distress and not identify with her.

> My client arrived very late explaining, as she sat down, that she had been staying overnight in London and was late because a bomb had exploded on the Underground. She went on to describe what had happened. I realized that the explosion had been at the tube station that my son used every day and that it had happened at the height of the morning rush hour. I do not know how I got through the 35 minutes that were left of her time. My heart was pounding, I felt sick and I could barely think. After the session ended I found to my relief a message on the answerphone to say my son was safe. It was only then that I sank to my knees and allowed myself to cry.

This therapist carried on with the session after she heard of the bomb. Others might have explained the situation to the client and closed it. Her inner resources were stretched to their limits.

The difficulty with our business is that no one can stand in for us. If we decide that we cannot work, our client does not have a session.

Well-being

It was suggested that I split this chapter into two; for example, that support and resources should be a separate subject from health considerations. This suggestion reflects the splitting between mind and body that can occur within the therapist. But it seems perfectly obvious to me that, in order to function well, we must take as much care of our physical health as our mental and psychological well-being. So I decided to include our need for physical maintenance in this chapter, recognizing that it is a crucial aspect of our support systems.

It is surprising how many therapists seem to ignore the need to care for their bodies and carry on as if physical robustness is of no consequence. It can almost sound like a badge of honour when a therapist describes herself as being completely exhausted, and a certain omnipotence can be detected when we talk about our seven-, eight-, nine- or even ten-hour day.

In the institution where I trained, I saw many therapists earnestly moving between rooms. Child therapists clutching cushions under their arms always looked the most exhausted, but many others also looked pale and preoccupied, their postures more often than not bent in concentration and leaning forward with a sense of purpose. It seemed to me that bodies were disregarded; everyone was too busy to take any notice of their physical needs.

Consider this; if we work an eight-hour day we are doing the equivalent of flying to New York from London. We sit as still as we would on a plane but unlike the traveller we are not relaxing, we are working hard, using all our concentration to understand what is happening in our consulting room. No wonder we look pale.

> It was the end of the summer break and many of my friends were returning to work at the same time. It was amazing; everyone I talked to was in bed by 8.30pm. It was as if the effort of picking up their workload had completely exhausted them. I know by next week we will all have settled into a routine and will be feeling fine, rather like a pack-horse that groans as it shoulders the weight and then forgets about it as it becomes a familiar load to carry.

It is a bit tough to compare yourself to a pack-horse, which does not have a choice about his load, but the anecdote serves to illustrate the weight that many therapists carry.

Even the therapist who works an eight-hour day will have a 10-minute break between clients. Time enough to do a bit of arm swinging, but how many of us do? If our day is so full that the 10 minutes between clients is all we have, it is more than likely that we will fill that space with domestic chores, which will squeeze out any possibility of exercise.

With a small amount of organization it might be possible to allow for more time between clients and a full hour for lunch. You might then choose to allocate your time to allow for the telephone calls that must be made, lunch and some exercise. It takes quite a lot of discipline to keep to a routine, because clients may need to change their times and we want to accommodate them as much as we can. But you will be moving some way to organizing a more healthy life simply by bringing your relentless schedule to consciousness.

Our business is particularly restricting. We cannot offer our clients another therapist if we feel unwell and we cannot, on the spur of the moment, decide that as it is a beautiful day we will postpone our work. We are immobilized for the period of time that we are with our clients. We cannot take a telephone call, answer the door or respond to a call of nature, though I dare say we would answer the call of nature if it was urgent enough!

Our weeks are prescribed for us by the timetable we set with clients. The routine, which remains so much the same from week to week, offers no time for spontaneous action and, as such, creates an utterly predictable pattern, which seems to make days and weeks pass at the speed of light. Given the fact that at the heart of our work is a commitment to regular sessions for our clients, there is very little we can do to vary our routine. We must therefore create within our working week space for us to look after ourselves. The longer the hours we work the more difficult it is to find time, but the more important it is to do so.

This is by definition setting ourselves another routine, which might be in danger of becoming a persecuting demand rather than a respite from work, but if you can build into your week some exercise and a nourishing meal in the middle of the day, you will feel surprisingly more energetic and become fitter.

It took me some time to realize that I was slowly but surely putting on weight. It was not difficult to understand why. In between clients I would drift into the kitchen; the bread, which was left permanently on the bread board, made it very convenient for me to absent-mindedly cut myself a slice to have with butter and jam. Delicious and comforting, but disastrous and, coupled with a complete lack of exercise, actually minus exercise as I sit so very still, I was piling on the weight at an alarming rate. It was worrying as I have heard recently of people of my age, with far less sedentary jobs than mine, who have had strokes and heart attacks. I decided to take myself in hand and have put the bread out of sight. I have a proper breakfast, which means I don't get so hungry, and I have paced out a walk that takes me half an hour to do. So far I can manage three walks a week, but I am working on taking more. I also make starting the walk easy by always having suitable shoes and coats available so that I can make a quick getaway and have no excuse not to go out.

There are countless ways that we can build in some sort of exercise for ourselves; it is just a matter of deciding we want to do it. We could find a friend to run with, take up yoga, buy a small trampoline, sweep the leaves . . . the list goes on, but none of it works until you decide you must pay attention to your body.

It is, however, undeniable that when it comes to resources and support, it is as important to look after your soma as it is to care for your psyche.

> I had an operation on my knee which really took its toll. I react badly to anaesthetic and needed far longer than most to recuperate. I was recovered well enough after six weeks or so, but didn't want to go back to seeing clients until I could put my foot down on the floor. A very experienced counsellor, whom I respect a great deal, wondered why I was being so fussy. 'After all,' she said, 'you will let your clients know that you are human if you show them that your knee is still not fully better.' She was quite right, but the fact is I did not want my clients to know I was 'human'; I wanted to show them that I was fully recovered and functioning at one hundred per cent.

This therapist is highlighting, with refreshing honesty, the omnipotence that we can all succumb to when working with clients. We take seriously our commitment to be reliably available to our clients and try our utmost not to disrupt their sessions by responding to our personal needs. But overconscientiousness can mean that we will not allow ourselves to pay attention to our own frailties and to admit that it might be better for us in the long run to cancel a session, rather than suffer through it with a temperature and sore throat or other symptoms.

It is remarkable how few sessions a therapist will cancel during the course of her career. Stamina and a commitment to our work is clearly a powerful combination which ensures the continuity so necessary in our business, but it should not be achieved at the cost of our own health.

The therapist who had the operation on her knee was entirely sensible not to think of returning to work until she was feeling strong, but she might have taken the risk of 'being human' and allowed her clients to see that she needed to rest her leg, without compromising the containing relationship she had with her clients.

The support that we can call upon is a mixture of the professional and personal. Through a combination of practical and psychological resources, we endeavour to be a safe pair of hands. When we see our clients we have the support of an invisible matrix of professional relationships, a containing network that ensures our clients have a safe environment in which to work.

7

Maintaining Your Practice

I bumped into an old friend of mine the other day. For a usually cheerful and optimistic soul she looked unusually glum. 'I seem', she said anxiously, 'to be terribly down on clients; last month I was inundated with referrals and thought I would not be able to fit them all in. In fact I turned a few away.' She turned pale at the thought. 'Now my practice seems to have evaporated, what with some people leaving and others not able to come at the times I have free – I will never again tell someone I cannot fit them in.

Being self-employed is a challenge; being a self-employed therapist with an established practice is particularly challenging. Unlike other self-employed professionals we are limited in the amount of work we can do; we cannot expand our business by bringing in more therapists to share our load. We cannot hand our client's file over to a colleague and ask her to stand in for us while we attend to other urgent business, and most of us do not have a secretary who can field questions or change appointments for us.

Because we understand that unconscious communication is such an important part of our work, we know that our clients will be affected by the smallest of deviations in our routine. We acknowledge this by working within tight boundaries and by maintaining a predictable presence and routine, which leaves us little room for spontaneous action and no scope to share our workload.

We have the freedom of the self-employed to choose how many hours a week we want to work, how much holiday we want to take and how to run our business, but freedom can become unnerving when we realize we have to fill the hours we want to work with clients, that we will have no income when we take a break and that our business, like any other business, requires us to fill in income tax returns, pay insurance premiums and comply with professional standards.

Paradoxically, we can capitalize on our autonomy best when we accept the constraints we are under and access our freedom from within the framework of our very particular business structures.

Feast or famine

Maintaining a viable and professionally rewarding practice can often seem a difficult balancing act. If we have too many clients we can feel overloaded and stressed; too few and we panic, worrying that our work is about to dry up completely.

As we decide how many hours we intend to work in a week there are a number of factors to take into consideration, some of which we have looked at in previous chapters. Our work, which is often demanding, can also be very rewarding and we might find ourselves committed to working long hours simply because we enjoy it. Our working schedule may fluctuate over the years according to our financial requirements and family commitments. Being able to expand and contract our practice according to our circumstances is one of the bonuses of being self-employed in general and being a self-employed therapist in particular.

Therapists work in many different ways. The length and depth of the work we do can vary enormously, from focused short-term counselling to open-ended psychoanalysis, but whichever way we work we will need to find a way of maintaining a viable practice, and that will mean juggling a wide variety of factors.

A psychoanalyst who sees clients three or four times a week will experience different demands on both her inner and outer resources than will a counsellor who is doing short-term work.

If you are seeing clients on average for six sessions, you will have a greater turnover of work, and therefore be more often concerned about where your next client will come from, than the psychoanalyst who enjoys the less volatile nature of long-term analytic work.

Your capacity to work a full face-to-face 30-hour week will depend very much on the number of clients you are seeing at any one time. A couple therapist would find it extremely difficult to see seven couples in a day whereas a psychoanalyst who regularly sees fewer clients three times a week might well be able to work a seven or eight-hour day.

To work with 30 couples each week, to hold 60 people in mind with troubled relationships, would be well-nigh impossible and a very different experience from holding 10 individuals in mind who you are seeing three times a week.

If you are an individual psychotherapist your practice may feel more secure than if you are a couple counsellor. To have a committed client in three-times-a-week psychotherapy is certainly more predictable than working with a couple, two people who might be on the verge of leaving both each other and their counsellor. But, conversely, when a couple leaves, you will only be losing one client hour, whereas when your long-term, three-times-a-week client finishes you will be losing the equivalent of three client hours in one fell swoop.

The number of hours we want to work, the nature of our work and whether our clients are couples, families, children or individuals will all inform the way we think about our practice and determine how we find a working pattern that works well for us.

A movable feast

Clients often ask us how long they can expect to be in therapy, and it is, of course, impossible to give a precise answer, but we do have the experience of our particular practice to rely on. Over time we will develop a sense of how long our clients might stay with us, which is a helpful yardstick for both us and our clients.

At the start of therapy it can be difficult to determine how the therapy will proceed so we respond to the anxieties and needs of our clients by being as flexible as we can within the therapeutic boundaries. A client might be extremely wary of becoming dependent on a therapist and resist any suggestions of coming to see you more than once a week, even if you think he would be best served by embarking straight away on twice-weekly sessions.

Someone you have seen for years may be working towards an ending, the date of which might be in both your diaries, but endings are not set in tablets of stone and you might think it wise to revise the decision and defer the ending, realizing as you do so that you will no longer have the free slot to offer that you thought you had.

A family therapist who usually sees each family once a week may respond to the way the work is going and offer them twice-weekly sessions; an individual client who you have been seeing three times a week may decide to reduce the number of sessions to two a week. Our working timetables can sometimes be very movable feasts and we often find ourselves balancing the need for continuity and commitment with the demands of both the internal and external worlds of our clients.

Our business model, which is predicated on regular and pre-dictable sessions, might have to take a back seat while we accom-modate our clients' own working schedules, but to be able to negotiate the delicate balance between the therapy world and the outside world is an important part of the work that we do and plays a vital role when it comes to filling and maintaining our practice.

Securing the business

A colleague referred a very high-powered businessman to me. 'He is known to be demanding and difficult,' she said, adding, seductively, 'you are the only person I can think of who will be able to manage him.' It took some weeks for my potential client and me to make contact. I had messages sent from airports and taxis left on my answerphone which meant he was incommunicado when I returned them. When we finally did manage to speak he told me he was so busy he thought it would be impossible for us to make a time to meet. He was very surprised, when he did find a time that he could see me, to find that I was not available to see him. Clearly there was only one busy person in his world, and it was not me.

We finally booked a session, which he cancelled the day before he was due. However, we persevered and arranged to meet the following week; this time he did keep the appointment but arrived half an hour early. I sensed the vulnerability of this 'very busy and important man' and contrary to my usual practice decided, as I was available, to see him before his appointed time.

This therapist did not let her irritation or frustration get in the way of negotiating a meeting with her new client. She conscientiously responded to the numerous telephone calls, did not take issue with his assumption that she was not busy, or challenge his cancellation of the session at such short notice. She also recognized this man's vulnerability by accommodating his early arrival.

Ensuring that we find new clients while engaging with our ongoing work is an essential part of our therapeutic business. We feel panicky if we think that our client level is dropping. From one week to the next we can go from feeling overwhelmed by work and inundated with enquiries to being alarmed as one client after another contemplates life without therapy. We must contain our anxiety at times like this, maintain our professional objectivity and think through with our clients their ambivalence about therapy, rather than persuade them to stay. Hanging on to clients is just not an option. It is at times like this that it seems as if the telephone never rings.

Most therapists from time to time feel worried about the viability of their practice. When we are feeling vulnerable and clients express dissatisfaction with us, it can sometimes be hard to remain confident about our work.

It is a curious fact of therapeutic life that clients do seem to come in clusters and that within the space of a week or two we can move from having too few clients to having too many.

Accepting that few of us ever truly feel that we have found the perfect balance between work and rest goes a long way to resolving our omnipotent fantasy that we can achieve it.

Taking a break

When we are feeling anxious about our client level it can feel a risky business to take a break, but if we are to maintain a functioning and viable practice we need to maintain a functioning practitioner.

It can be very difficult to decide to cancel clients if we are feeling unwell, from the point of view both of disrupting the work and of losing income. There can be omnipotence in our desire to carry on regardless. I have known therapists who literally drag themselves out of bed in order to see their clients, refusing to acknowledge that they have a fever or are in too much pain to be able to think properly.

> I look back on a time when I had the flu; having taken a week off, I decided enough was enough and that although I was still feeling terribly unwell I ought to get back to work. I managed a full working week by watching television in between clients; I never watch daytime TV, but it enabled me to switch off completely between sessions, thus allowing me to carry on. In retrospect I do not know who I was carrying on for, myself or my clients, but whatever the reason it was completely ridiculous to do so. With hindsight I think a two-week break would have been beneficial for both me and my clients. They would have had the experience of a therapist who could look after herself, and I would have got better

much more quickly. As it was it took me ages to recover my health and strength.

We need to weigh up the pros and cons of taking a break when we are ill, but unfortunately it is at just such a time as this that we are least able to take a rational decision. Our clients' reactions can vary from being completely oblivious to our illness, to such deep concern about our indisposition that they cannot concentrate on anything else. While some clients may appreciate a stoical therapist who carries on with a streaming cold, others might worry that they will catch it.

We cannot always predict how long we will be ill for and can be forgiven, even applauded, for being optimistic about our powers of recovery. But it is not shameful to occasionally call it quits and take to one's bed. Sometimes it is the most therapeutic thing to do for all concerned.

We cannot plan when to have the flu or a ruptured appendix, but we can plan for an elective operation. It is then possible to prepare your clients for your break. You may or may not choose to tell them why you will be absent, depending on the circumstances, but it is important to be clear about the length of time you will be away and when you will return.

I knew my therapist was going to have an operation, she told me she would probably be taking ten weeks off and we put a date in the diary for my sessions to resume. I was resigned to the long break and therefore rather surprised, but pleased, when she telephoned me to let me know that the operation went well and that she hoped to return to work sooner than expected. However, I received another telephone call two weeks later, to say that she was feeling really exhausted and would not after all be resuming her work sooner than expected, in fact she was going to take rather longer to recuperate than previously thought. I was confused. I knew I should be feeling sympathetic towards my therapist, but I was furious and felt completely messed about.

This client had a right to feel angry. Rather than the therapist containing her client it sounds as if she was expecting the client to contain her. There was no need for this client to be party to the ups and downs of her therapist's recovery. It would have been better if there had been a generous amount of time allowed for recuperation, with the therapist accommodating any deviation to what had been expected to happen.

Taking a sabbatical

> I worried terribly about taking a six-month break. I could not see how I would manage to keep my very full practice going if I left my clients for such a long time, but I had the chance to accompany my husband to Africa on a sabbatical and I really wanted to go, so I decided to take the risk. I was able to give my clients a year's notice and I used the coming break to think with them about their particular relationship to loss, to absence and in one case to betrayal of trust. After a wonderful break I returned to work with renewed enthusiasm. I did not lose one client in the process.

As long as the break is planned for and you prepare your clients well in advance for your absence, even a six-month sabbatical does not need to be detrimental to your practice.

An unconscious choice

> A number of years ago I saw a young woman for an initial consultation. She had been advised to consult a number of therapists in order to find the one most suitable for her. She was not English and she wondered if it might be best to see someone who spoke her 'mother tongue'. This seemed to be terribly important and I wondered if it was connected to her mother who had died in tragic circumstances when she was a small child. Although I did not speak her 'mother tongue' she came back several weeks later

having decided to work with me. I wondered with her on her choice of therapist; she was only able to say that I seemed to be just right.

Over the next year or so she told the story of her mother's death but she was unable to remember anything about her. Her father had thought it best never to speak of her mother or how she died. One day my client brought a photograph of her mother and herself as a baby 'to prove she really existed'. As I glanced down at the photograph I was completely shocked and bewildered. I think I am looking at a photograph of myself as a young woman, the same facial features, distinctive hair and similar body posture. I look at this picture of a lovely young woman smiling out from the photograph, with her arms around her little girl, and I realize that my client has found herself a therapist who is a close match to the mother she has not yet been able to bring to mind.

This tender story reminds us in a particularly graphic way of the large part the unconscious plays in the business of therapy.

Your professional community

Ours is a profession where it is important to keep on developing. Our clients unconsciously recognize when a therapist has become stuck and jaded. That is why continuing professional development (CPD) is so important; it is central to keeping one's work up to the minute and relevant.

Although CPD is now a formalized requirement for our profession, good therapists have always been committed to deepening and developing an understanding of the work they do. To attend conferences and other informative events not only ensures that we maintain professional standards, it also provides a forum for us to interact with colleagues, a network which is vital for the continuing life of our practice.

> I have always found it essential to build links with my professional organization – serving on committees, being a tutor or teaching. These activities can be the lifeblood of our profession. As our career progresses and our practice matures they provide the opportunity to link up regularly with other and often more experienced members of our profession.

We looked at the need to be part of a professional community when we were considering the development of a new practice. When we are no longer newcomers we have much to give to our profession, and in so doing find ourselves involved and sustained by a wealth of friends and colleagues. By serving on committees, supervising and teaching we help to create a thriving community and raise the profile of our work. The more we do, the more we will be asked to do, and if we are willing to participate in the development of our profession without groaning about our onerous duties, we will be regarded as a reliable and valuable colleague. The gains to personal development are great when we throw ourselves into the work of our societies. It is so much better to get on and help when we are needed than to complain that we are overworked and expected to do something for no financial reward.

> I often have trainees or newly qualified practitioners contact me for referrals, but I tell them I do not refer to anyone whose work I do not know.

What better way to ensure that you are known and therefore referred to than to be a fully committed member of your professional community. You will also find that as your contribution to the business of therapy increases, so will the material for your website, the updating of which is now crucial to maintaining a presence and developing a reputation in the community at large.

As you become established in your area your clients will begin to act as a referral system, often giving your name to their friends who are looking for a therapist. There are advantages and disadvantages to being known, particularly if your community is small and you have been working in it for a long time.

> I no longer go to dance classes or anything of an alternative nature; I have had several uncomfortable encounters which I would choose to avoid. I have from time to time run into clients at the local gym and chosen not to undress in the changing rooms. It is one thing to run into a client in gym trousers, quite another to meet them in a state of undress.

As the years go by the rich mulch of clients, friends and colleagues can be challenging to confidentiality, so it is up to us to maintain the boundaries and make sure that the trust of clients, both past and present, is not betrayed.

Mistakes

> Sometimes I think there should be a prize for the therapist who can get dressed in the shortest time. It should not of course ever happen, but who among us has never been woken by the bell heralding our early morning client? Did I sleep through the alarm or didn't it go off – the thoughts race at the speed of light through my frantic mind, as I hurl a jumper over my head, throw toothpaste in the general direction of my mouth and abandon all thoughts of encasing shaking legs into unyielding tights. Fighting for calm, three minutes later I open the door to my 7.15am client. I struggle to find an internal thinking space, hoping that my client does not notice my pounding heart.

As our practice matures and we consolidate our position as a good practitioner in both our professional and lay community, we will no doubt cringe as we think of mistakes we have made and wish we could try again as we remember opportunities we have missed and situations we have mismanaged. We work hard with our clients to bring difficult situations to consciousness and challenge their defences when they deny the harmful effects of their actions on others, so it is not surprising that it is not possible for us to relegate our mistakes to the oblivion of our unconscious.

> I am not a paragon of virtue, but I don't think I have made a lot of bloomers. I have never opened the door to a patient in my pyjamas, but I have opened the door thinking it was one person and then seen another on the step. I have wondered if my face gave away something of the shock. Many years ago I double-booked a regular patient and a new referral. When they both arrived on the doorstep at the same time I had no alternative but to apologize to the new person and admit to making an error. She was charming and understanding, but when I contacted her to rearrange her appointment she had decided to see someone else.

There is little room for error in our profession. The conscious and urbane part of this new patient was able to be reasonable and accommodating by leaving without a fuss, but she had unconsciously registered the muddle as a rejection and voted with her feet. The therapist was in a double bind: she had no choice but to respond to the patient's conscious communication, but unless she was able to speak to the unconscious rejection that her new patient had suffered she had little chance of keeping her. Because there was no therapeutic container in place, it was not possible to make the interpretation that would have saved the day.

Enactments

> I was frustrated and in a terrible hurry. I had numerous bags and, in something of a temper with head down, I tried to squeeze past

someone who was blocking my way on the escalator. I managed to overtake the irritating shopper, but then tripped and landed on the shop floor amidst the contents of my bags. I was helped to my feet by a charming young man, but imagine my dismay when I found that my rescuer was my client. I had been seeing this client for some time and his therapy was going well. He had worked hard to understand his relationship with his mother, who was immature and had caused him deep anxiety as a child. He had spent much of his childhood trying to protect his mother from careless and sometimes destructive behaviour. At a very early age he became the parent to an inadequate mother.

After my client had rescued me from the shop floor our work became very difficult. I embodied all that he had hated and mistrusted in his mother, her carelessness and inability to look after herself had been re-enacted by me at the top of the escalator. He was furious – his therapist had turned out to be as unreliable as his mother. Although this put the relationship between my client and me under a lot of pressure it enabled us to revisit the work we had done,

but this time in a truly dynamic way. The rescue on the shop floor was the turning point in my client's therapy.

We can never orchestrate these coincidental occurrences, but when there is an unconscious enactment of such magnitude it may prove to be a therapeutic gift.

It can take many years to feel confident enough of our professional ability to be able to use our fallibility and realize that mistakes often reveal something important but unconscious in the working dynamic between client and therapist. It is often the mistakes that move the therapy along, but only if the therapeutic boundaries are firmly in place.

But can we say 'No'?

Having urged you to participate fully in the activities of your professional community I want to add a cautionary note. When we are working to our full capacity seeing clients, supervising work, sitting on committees, writing papers or even books, we may from time to time find that we are overwhelmed. It can then be helpful to take stock of our workload and if possible reduce it, before we start to act out in unhelpful ways.

I agreed to see a supervisee, who was living a long way away, on a Saturday morning once a month. She had to start her journey very early in the morning to get to me for a 10.00am appointment and I had to remember to mark that Saturday morning off from my normally free weekends. I have a very busy practice and I think part of me was not happy with this arrangement on a long-term basis, but I wanted to oblige the supervisee who was convinced she could not find a suitable supervisor in her area or come during the week. One Saturday morning, after about a year of this arrangement, I forgot her session and opened the door, still in my pyjamas, to find a rather angry supervisee on my doorstep. Although I quickly got dressed and we had the session with a later start, my unconscious mistake made my supervisee think again and she decided to seek out supervision nearer to home. I think this was the right decision for both parties, but I had been unaware of any resentment on my part until I enacted it.

Trust your work and your colleagues

Private practice is not for the fainthearted, but then therapists do not suffer from faint hearts. We do not shy away from the difficult aspects of life and are robust in our determination to seek the truth and to challenge our client's defences, which can often keep us from it.

We should trust that our predictability and commitment to clients, our continuing investment in professional development and our input into the profession as a whole will ensure that we have a thriving practice. When you are low on clients, let your colleagues know; when you are ill or tired try to take a rest; and be generous to your profession, which is the lifeblood of your work.

8

Endings

I have given much thought to the business of ending. I realize that I do now have a feeling of increased vulnerability. As I approach the end of my career I am beginning to be aware of my fallibility and my own ending. I think this means that my clients' projections hit me in rather a different way. I have become more sensitive to them and less able to separate my feeling self from my thinking mind. There seems to be a thinner membrane now between my unconscious and conscious. This is an advantage, provided I am aware of what is happening and am still able to think. I was not surprised when one of my clients began to have dreams about her mother dying. I am sure that this was linked to the possibility of me dying. Because I was able consciously to make these connections, it created an opportunity for my client to work through some of her deepest unconscious fears of losing her mother.

This therapist highlights the conundrum of becoming older in our business. On the one hand our advancing years can be an advantage to both us and our clients, 'provided I am aware of what is happening and am still able to think'. If, however, we are not 'still able to think', our seniority can be a hazard.

Illness and incapacity can be an interruption to the predictable pattern of our working lives, whether it is the therapist or the client who is ill. Our business consists entirely of the human interaction of a particular client and his particular therapist. The success of the work depends on both participants turning up. Neither can have a stand-in if they are indisposed. As therapists, it is up to us to manage and contain any interruptions to the flow of the work.

Dilemmas

My two clients had more than their fair share of problems. Mr M was undergoing treatment for a debilitating illness at the same time as running a business which was in trouble. Mrs M was looking after the home and the children but also trying to find work, having been made redundant. Money was very tight and I acknowledged this by seeing them for a lower than usual fee. I saw them for six months, each week seeming to highlight more problems than the last. The stress this couple was under was terrible and I worried that the benefits of the therapy were being outweighed by the cost. I was not charging them for missed sessions and considered waiving my fees altogether, but after much thought I decided it would not be helpful to do so.

In retrospect I think this was the right decision because, when eventually Mrs M found work, it was clear that the logistics of coping with children, jobs and hospital visits meant that it was too difficult for them to manage the sessions, regardless of having more money. I think it was important for this couple to come to terms with the limitations of their resources.

Life is tough

The above therapist would not have been able to alleviate the suffering of her clients even if she had offered them sessions free of charge. The clients were fighting on all fronts to find a way to survive; the therapist recognized that they had to look after their financial and physical problems before they could turn their attention to their relationship; both she and her clients saw the limitations of the therapeutic work. Occasionally we do have to acknowledge that therapy might not be the most important aspect of our clients' lives. The most therapeutic response to an agonizing situation might be to support a client's decision to leave therapy.

> I was in therapy with a very experienced psychotherapist who had come highly recommended. After the death of my mother, who I had looked after for years, I became very depressed. I am an only child and have always taken responsibility for my parents. Now they were both dead I felt utterly bereft. I felt my therapist was really in tune with me and that I could at last unburden myself to someone who understood me, but after about a year it became apparent that my analyst was very unwell. Before I knew it I found myself supporting her just as I had my mother. The therapy did not come to a proper ending; one day my therapist telephoned me to say she could not see me at the usual time and that she would ring to let me know when next to come. I never heard from her again; she died a few weeks later.

When this psychotherapist became ill, the dynamic between her and her client changed and came to resemble the relationship the client had had with her parents. In the transference the client became once again the responsible child, sympathetic and supportive to her sick and seemingly dependent therapist, who she had grown so fond of. Her therapist was too ill to interpret the all-important transference, which would have enabled this client to understand the role she habitually took with people. Her role as the responsible child/parent got acted out yet again. An opportunity was missed.

This psychotherapist was also caught up in the transference and, no doubt because she was very unwell, was unable to take a decision that would have been in the best interests of her client. The psychological and emotional demands of our work are great, which is why we put so many safeguards in place, why we have a network of professional help to turn to. When we become gravely ill, it is understandable that our capacity to hold our boundaries can become weak. If we are told that we have a terminal illness, we may be forgiven for losing our capacity, at least for a while, to be able to think. Paradoxically it is when we need our professional peer group most that we may be least able to access them both physically and emotionally.

As we and our peers get older we are increasingly vulnerable to a multitude of ailments.

The notion of becoming incapacitated in any way is alarming and most of us believe, quite understandably, that it will not happen to us, but just in case it does we can look out for each other and, if we suspect one of us is suffering and continuing to see clients, we should have the courage to raise the alarm and suggest ways of helping.

Interruptions

Interestingly, I found it far harder to deal with my clients after the short break I took when my husband died than I did when I took a three-month sabbatical. Most of my clients knew of my loss and many felt it was insensitive to speak about their own worries when I had problems of my own. This doubled my work, as I had not only to deal with my grief but also with my clients' fantasies about what I was feeling.

Clients can be acutely sensitive to their therapist's state of mind. They may as children have spent years tuning into an emotionally absent mother, as a consequence of which they spend a lot of therapeutic time trying to tune into their therapist.

I had been in therapy for about three years and making some progress in dealing with my acute shyness. One day my therapist told me that she was going to take a sabbatical when my therapy came to an end. I did not discuss with her what she meant but I assumed she was desperate for a break and the only thing between her and

six months on a beach somewhere was me. I decided to end my
therapy there and then and I left a month later. Well, I can take a hint.

This shy client did not stick around to find out what his therapist
meant when she told him she was planning a sabbatical. He
interpreted her words as a rejection and decided to leave her
before she could leave him. This sad tale reminds us why we
put so much emphasis on and pay close attention to a client's
decision to finish therapy. Endings are very difficult for us all to
bear. Therapists and clients alike have many defences in place to
avoid the pain of separation.

During the course of a long career we will work with many
endings, some more painful than others. One of my supervisees,
who is retiring, has worked hard in supervision to deal with the
difficulty of processing both the ending of her clients' therapies
and her own career. It has been a difficult time for her, but she has
held on to her therapeutic hat and continued to be able to think
through the often painful process of saying 'goodbye' to so many
clients. 'But there is one couple', she said wistfully, 'who I will be

so sorry to end with, they are just the sort of people who, under different circumstances, I could be friends with.' My supervisee is highlighting how upsetting it can be to say goodbye to the clients with whom we feel we have a special affinity.

Over the years we will encounter many interruptions to our personal life that may threaten to disrupt the smooth running of our practice and face us with dilemmas of how best to manage them. We have explored our resources, both professional and personal, in a previous chapter and thought about how to make use of them. We may have coped with children leaving home, builders, noisy neighbours, a move of consulting room – a thousand small irritations – but whatever the problems, they were dealt with as part of the maelstrom of a busy and active life. It can feel as if the 'slings and arrows of outrageous fortune' are more lethal as we get older, when it is inevitable that we will have to cope with more illness and death among those nearest to us. As elders we are dealing with difficult and painful situations within a life that feels finite rather than infinite. We view our professional work decisions from a different perspective, a perspective that has more history than future.

A change of plan

Be open to surprises. I took early retirement from the institute in which I had worked for many years. I planned to paint and to cruise my barge on the canals of Britain but, in the event, I found that I was in demand as a consultant to organizations. I had absolutely no intention of being self-employed but chose to do whatever turned up. And I have had a ball. I now realize that I could not possibly have afforded to do my painting and cruising without some sort of an income to supplement my pension. As it is, I make sure I have plenty of time for my boat but I also go with the flow and accept as much work as I want to do. It is great – I do not plan to retire again anytime soon.

This therapist, who had been well known and respected for her work with couples and groups in the social services arena, found herself in demand as a consultant to organizations after she had retired. She struck a good balance between work and pleasure, and one which can be maintained throughout 'retirement'.

A fortunate profession

To retire or not to retire becomes an increasingly hot topic of conversation as we and our peer group get older. There is no compulsory age of retirement for practitioners in private practice which, for many of the reasons we have looked at, can be both a help and a hindrance. If we have our wits about us there is no reason why we should not carry on practising our craft well into old age. After all, wisdom is the prerogative of the old. But there can be a fine line between a wise practitioner who uses the experience of many years of work to good effect and a self-styled guru.

The advantages of being self-employed in our profession are that we do not have to stop practising completely unless we are incapacitated. It is possible to have more free time and continue to see clients, but we need to think about how we schedule our new routine; it often helps to talk to those colleagues and friends who are in the same boat as we are.

There are many practical issues to be considered when we are thinking about retirement, not least of which is our pension. This is generally a very vexed question, particularly at this time. For the majority, the business of therapy is not one in which we are able to accumulate great wealth. We cannot franchise ourselves or market our product or retire while someone else does the work. Our private pension, even if we have contributed to it from the outset, is unlikely to yield more than a modest income, certainly not a large one. It is therefore unsurprising that some therapists postpone their retirement year after year.

Many who have always worked privately have not paid enough National Insurance contributions to accumulate a good state pension. Unless, when we were young and immortal, we have been given good pension advice and taken it, or have a partner who has a company pension, we will inevitably, as we get older, come face to face with the alarming question of how to survive and live a good life into old age.

If our best option is to continue to do some work in order to subsidize a pension, we can be grateful that our profession offers us the opportunity to work for as long as we want or are able to. Because we are accustomed to dealing with the insecurity of self-employment, we are well placed to develop and enjoy the fluid structure that a working retirement can bring. We are used to managing the highs and lows and shifting pattern of private practice; this is a very different situation from those who have been used to the security of employment in an organization and have to face compulsory retirement.

> I am always bumping into colleagues these days who ask me anxiously if I am still working. When I say 'yes' they visibly relax. We sometimes go on to say 'because I cannot afford to retire' but the words do not have to be spoken, one can recognize a fellow traveller.

A working retirement

There are many options open to us if we choose to engage in a working retirement. We might decide to reduce the hours we work in a day, or think it better to reduce the days on which we see clients. We could choose to reduce the amount of time we work incrementally, allowing time for a natural diminution of clients to take place if we do not take on new cases for a while; or, once we have taken the plunge and decided to work less, we might want to change our schedule straight away.

When the decision is made and you have set out a clear course to follow, I imagine that your new pattern of work will fall easily into place. If you are unsure about your new plan of action and not clear about your goal, it will be more difficult to achieve a satisfactory solution. You need to think through what you are planning to do. Decide what you need to earn, taking into account the reduced amount of income tax you will have to pay if you are earning less. Think about how you will use your extra free time. Whatever you are planning to do – enrol on a course, look after the grandchildren or just lie on a sofa eating grapes – it will help you to decide whether to work a shorter day or a shorter week if you can anticipate your newfound freedom and how you want to use it.

A critical mass

When you reduce your hours it is important to retain a critical mass of client work. If you work too few hours you will find that when, as inevitably happens, your client base shifts and you suddenly lose two or three client hours, you are left with too little work to be either satisfactory or viable. If you do not reduce your hours enough you will lose out on the value of working less and simply become frustrated with a practice that is neither full nor part time.

If you have been working a full five-day week and cut down to three days you will, at least initially, feel as if you are on holiday and still be able to see clients more than once a week if you want to. Reducing to three days a week also leaves room to reduce your work by one more day, if and when it seems appropriate. Should you choose to work fewer hours in the day, it is best to decide to work either in the morning or in the afternoon, and put a time in the diary beyond which you will not go, and then stick to it. It is easier to go 'off piste' if you are reducing the working hours in the day rather than the working days in the week.

You may decide that longer breaks would work best for you; this is a perfectly sensible arrangement as long as you let your clients know in the first consultation what to expect. Clients can then choose whether to engage with you or not. The type of work you take on might change if you work this way, as it will be difficult to contain fragile clients if you plan on taking very long breaks.

> I no longer see patients but continue to do supervision of qualified counsellors and psychotherapists. However, I no longer see trainees as they would need and should have regular sessions.

This therapist has not quite gone cold turkey. By choosing to do some supervision, but not counsel trainees, she has freed herself from the discipline of regular hours that the business of therapy requires of us, but retained just enough work to keep her in the professional loop. This is an intelligent interim step before making the decision to stop work altogether.

Full retirement

You may spend a few years winding down by working part time, or you may decide to move from full-time work into full retirement. Either way, once you have decided to stop work completely there is much to consider.

> Retiring from being a therapist is a tough challenge because, while it is a relief not to have one's day regulated and controlled, you give up a fascinating occupation and lose the sense of yourself as a professional person. As the relationship with patients is the focus of the work, when you retire you have to take back all the projections and investments in relationships which have meaning and importance for yourself as well as for the patients.

Planning ahead

How much notice of your retirement you will need to give your clients will depend on how you work. Short-term clients do not require as much notice as those who you are seeing on a regular open-ended basis. You will want to give long-term clients as much time as possible to prepare for the process of ending. You will want to think through your impending retirement carefully before you let clients and colleagues know of your decision.

It is best not to discuss your thoughts on retirement openly with colleagues; if you do it can become a *fait accompli* before you have made a firm decision. Your existing clients may hear rumours, which will be distressing for them, and new clients could be deterred from approaching you.

> If one does long-term, open-ended work, then the plan to retire has to be made a long time ahead, perhaps as much as two years. This is especially so if one has a training role and works with trainees who have to qualify or need time to find a new therapist or supervisor. No more 'babies' might be the right decision but it is also one which contains feelings of loss and, inevitably, the confronting of a complete end . . . Death.

This therapist highlights the powerful feelings that can be evoked as we contemplate the ending of our career which, if we have invested many years in the development of a rewarding professional life, can be hard to give up.

It is much more difficult for us to retire from our, usually, satisfying work when we have little to replace it with. It is sobering to see therapists who continue to work because they have little else to do. We are arguably most effective as practitioners when we are not completely consumed by the work. It pays us to create and maintain other interests at all times and never more so than when we are coming up to retirement.

> I planned my retirement carefully and had a wonderful party to celebrate with colleagues and friends my thirty- five years as a thera-pist. I was nevertheless rather anxious about how I would manage without seeing my clients and enjoying the predictability and

structure of a working day. After all, I had followed a strict routine for years. I thought I might miss my clients terribly and worried that I might not get up in the mornings without the discipline of work. As it happens, I am having the most wonderful time. My life is filled with friends, gardening and visits to art galleries. The freedom to do what I want, when I want is absolutely marvellous.

I am definitely nearer the end of my career than the beginning and many of the conversations I have with colleagues revolve around the questions that I have raised in this chapter. Among older therapists, the question whether to retire occupies much of our thinking time and throws our minds into a maelstrom of possibilities, which can range from great delight to bleak loneliness. A friend of mine told me the other day that as she walked into her consulting room she thought, 'What would it be like coming into this room and not having any clients to see?' Before I could venture a response she laughed and said, 'Well, I could have time to prepare for Christmas!'

As we get older and the time ahead of us is getting shorter, the relentlessness of the schedules that our work demands from us can feel terribly restricting. The regularity of the sessions and predictability of the week make the months fly by incredibly quickly, just when we might want the passage of time to be slowing down a little. On the other hand, the challenges we encounter with our clients keep us on our toes. The timelessness of the therapeutic session can be reassuring, and wrestling with the complexities of a client's internal world while engaging with their presenting problem keeps our mind agile. Ours is not a boring profession.

We have spent many years helping clients to shine a bright light into the shadowy recesses of their minds and enabled them to understand their unconscious processes. We have helped them to recognize their ambivalence and to make decisions from a place of consciousness. As we approach the end of our careers we must do the same for ourselves.

In spite of my deciding to retire at a moment in time chosen by me, rather than determined by events and circumstances outside my control, I am still feeling a deep sense of sadness. I am aware of this alongside the feelings of relief and rightness of the decision. So I find myself wishing it was over and done with, while also wishing that it was not about to happen and that there was more time to go on enjoying my work. Knowing that retirement is what I have chosen and need to do, does not make it easy.

Although this therapist has thought long and hard about her reasons for retiring and reached a clear decision, she does nevertheless recognize the ambivalence she feels. She is looking forward to a rather exciting future but regrets the loss of a rewarding career. Retirement, for most of us, is not easy.

No gold clock

Although momentous to us, our retirement will have little impact on the outside world. Our business, which has always been conducted behind closed doors and maintained a low profile, will not create any headlines in the local newspaper when it closes down.

Unless we have been famous like Lionel Logue, the speech therapist who helped the stricken King George VI to find his voice and speak to his people, the success of our work will be acknowledged between us and our clients within the confines of our rooms, but rarely celebrated in the outside world.

We are unable to claim our successes or reveal the identity of our clients, and it is rare for a client to acknowledge publicly the help he has had from a therapist. We may briefly be an important part of our clients' lives but we relinquish our connection with them when the therapy ends. For the most part we do not know how our clients' lives will be after they have left us; we hope and trust that the work will be of lasting help and importance to them, but we rarely know for sure if it will be.

We cannot boast about our successes or bask in the reflected glory of our clients. We do not see our 'babies' grow up and are not party to their lives when they leave us. None of our clients will give us a gold clock when we retire, and if there is to be a farewell party, we will probably organize it ourselves.

A quiet affair

So our retirement is a quiet affair. We cannot sell our business on, claim our triumphs or receive public recognition for our work. We have committed a working lifetime to a profession which prides itself on integrity and confidentiality, protocols which do not cease when we close our doors to clients.

Much of the satisfaction of our work has been found in a close connection with colleagues and a rich professional life but, if we

have planned our retirement well, the liberation that retirement brings will surely compensate for the losses. A few colleagues will become lasting friends.

Our work gives us unique access into understanding the complexities of other people's lives. Through hours of therapeutic work we have helped clients to understand their inner worlds and in so doing we have developed a deep understanding of ourselves; a legacy from the extraordinary business of therapy, which is hard to quantify but which is, I suspect, far more valuable than a gold clock.

Index

access, therapy room
  practical considerations, 5–7
  see also specific considerations e.g.
    doorbells
Access to Personal Files Act
  (1987), 58
accuracy
  importance in taking of
    professional notes, 57–9
administration, business
  need and importance of business
    insurance, 60–61
  need and importance of income
    tax, 61–2
  need and importance of
    professional wills, 59–60
  see also elements e.g. data,
    protection of; paperwork,
    business
age
  impact on work as therapist,
    120–23
  see also outcomes of e.g.
    retirement
airiness and cleanliness
  importance in relation to therapy
    room, 11–12
appearances, therapist
  importance of smartness and
    neatness, 16
appointments, client
  need for flexibility, 107–10

arrangements, working
  features, strengths, and
    weaknesses of institutional,
    17–18
  features, strengths, and
    weaknesses of shared, 16–17
  limitations of possibility to alter,
    19–20
  see also environments, work; self-
    employment
artefacts
  protocols concerning receipt or
    use, 78–9
  see also invitations, client
assessment
  appropriate engagement at initial
    meeting, 33–4
  length and sensitivity of initial,
    34–6
audits, paper trail
  importance of maintaining
    regular, 67–8

bathrooms
  importance of appearance and
    location, 10
bells (doorbells)
  need to make decisions
    concerning interruptions by,
    7–9
bills and billing, client
  procedure and recording of, 43–5

boundaries, therapist-client
  danger and consequences when
      accepting invitations, 87–8
  essentiality of no breaches
      of, 85
  implications for therapy of
      crossing , 79–80
  importance in relation to session
      times, 76–8
  importance of for successful
      therapy, 48–9
  importance of setting during
      telephone calls, 82–3
  see also factors impacting
      e.g. curiosity, therapist;
      'dependent' therapist;
      familiarity, therapist-client;
      interest, therapist; nosiness,
      therapist; openness, therapist-
      client; promotion, self-
breaks and holidays see holidays
  and breaks
businesses, therapy
  considerations of home as
      location for, 62–3
  features of institutions as
      location for, 17–18
  importance of CPD as element
      of, 64
  strengths and weaknesses of
      shared practices, 16–17
  see also elements e.g.
      administration, business;
      insurance, business; marketing;
      paperwork, business
  see also factors affecting e.g.
      decisions, making of; events,
      external; holidays and breaks;
      illness and incapacity; time,
      therapist
  see also nature of e.g. self-
      employment

calls, telephone
  handling of crisis calls, 83–4
  importance of clarity and
      boundary setting during,
      82–3
  need for thoughtful and
      considered responses,
      81–2
cards, business
  requirement for and
      specifications, 54–5
cash
  strengths and weaknesses as fee
      payment method, 46–7
clarity
  importance during telephone
      calls, 82–3
  importance of therapy room
      signposting, 5–7
cleanliness and airiness
  importance in relation to therapy
      room, 11–12
clients, therapy
  considerations when embarking
      upon obtaining, 22–3
  impact of therapist schedule
      breaks on, 110–12
  impact of variability of numbers
      of, 106–7
  importance of approach to on
      retirement, 128–9
  importance of therapist first
      impressions of, 13–14,
      23–5
  need for appropriate initial
      engagement, 32–3
  need for flexibility as to
      schedules of, 107–10
  need for therapist to refrain from
      support from, 96–7
  procedures at first encounter
      with therapist, 31–2

process of finding, 25–6
see also boundaries, therapist-
client; commitment, client;
dissatisfaction, client
see also aspects affecting e.g.
confidentiality, client; fees;
privacy, client
see also sources of obtaining
e.g. registers, professional;
websites; Yellow Pages
see also types e.g. couples, client
clinics
strengths, and weaknesses of
working in, 17–18
cloakrooms
importance of appearance and
location, 10
closure, therapy
importance of acknowledging
need for, 121–3
need to handle appropriately,
123–5
codes, ethics
salience and importance in
therapy practice, 64–6
comfort and support, therapist
importance for refreshment
and self development,
93–4
importance of extraneous and
appropriate, 98–9
need to refrain from
inappropriate, 96–7
see also sources e.g. events,
external; families and friends;
peers
see also specific e.g. families and
friends; peers; practitioners,
general
commitment, client
importance of for successful
therapy, 48–9

conferences
importance for refreshment and
self development, 93–4
salience and importance of
attending, 114–15
confidentiality, client
salience and importance in
paperwork, 59
consultation, rooms for see therapy
rooms
continuing professional
development (CPD)
need for and recording of, 64
see also tools e.g. conferences;
meetings, therapy
couples, client
special requirements for working
with, 84–5
CPD (continuing professional
development)
need for and recording of, 64
see also tools e.g. conferences;
meetings, therapy
curiosity, therapist
dangers and consequences of, 86

data, protection of
essentiality for client data, 66
see also aspects subject to e.g.
e-mails; letters
Data Protection Act (1984), 58
decisions, making of
role of unconsciousness, 112–13
'dependent' therapist
danger and consequences of,
85–6
detachment, therapist
capacity of therapist for
maintenance of, 89–90
development, continuing
professional
need for and recording of, 64

directions, therapy location
importance of clarity and supply
of, 5–7
disabled
importance of therapy room
access for, 6
dissatisfaction, client
salience of therapist training in
fact of, 90–91
doorbells, interruptions by
need to make decisions
concerning, 7–9

EAP (Employment Assisted
Programme), 23
education, continuing
need for and recording of, 64
e-mails
need for thoughtful and
considered responses, 81–2
pre-requisites for appropriate, 67
empathy, therapist
capacity of therapist for
maintenance of, 89–90
Employment Assisted Programme
(EAP), 23
enactments
salience for self-employed practice,
116–18
endings, therapy
importance of acknowledging
need for, 121–3
need to handle appropriately,
123–5
entrances, practice
importance of appearance, 9–10
environments, work
characteristics of, 16–18
importance of clarity of
directions to, 5–7
need for practical preparatory
decision-making, 2–4

see also specific environments
e.g. therapy rooms; waiting
rooms
see also specific considerations and
practicalities e.g. cleanliness
and airiness; doorbells,
interruptions by; entrances,
practice; peacefulness; toilets
ethics
salience and importance in
therapy practice, 64–6
events, external
importance for refreshment and
self development, 93–4
salience and importance of
attending, 114–15
exercise, therapist
salience and organisation for
good health, 100–103

failure, therapy
importance of acknowledging,
121–3
familiarity, therapist-client
need for in sessions only, 73–6
see also boundaries, therapist-
client; dependence, therapist-
client
families and friends
role as source for comfort and
refreshment, 97–100
fees, client
gauging level and increase of,
39–41
importance of acknowledging
need for, 37–8
need for periodic review, 42–3
need to handle tactfully at initial
meeting, 34–6
see also procedures involved
e.g. bills and billing, client;
payments, fee

flexibility, schedule
  salience in relation to client
    appointments, 107–10
  salience in relation to client
    numbers, 106–7
friends and families
  role as source for comfort and
    refreshment, 97–100

general practitioners (GPs)
  role as source for comfort and
    advice, 94–5
gifts
  protocols concerning receipt or
    use, 78–9
  see also invitations, client
Green Door, The (Hodson), xvii–xx

halls, practice entrance
  importance of appearance, 9–10
health and well–being
  need and importance of
    maintenance of, 100–104
  see also means e.g. exercise,
    therapist; holidays and breaks;
    refreshment, therapist
Hodson, P., xvii–xx
holidays and breaks
  importance following illness,
    110–12
  need for policies on payment for,
    49–51
  see also specific e.g. sabbaticals
home, of therapist
  considerations as business
    location, 62–3

illness and incapacity, therapist
  importance of break and
    recuperation, 110–12
  impact on work as therapist,
    120–23

see also outcomes of e.g.
  retirement
impressions, of therapists
  importance to client of
    appropriate and prepared,
    13–14
income, taxing of
  need and importance, 61–2
increases, client fees
  need for and gauging levels of,
    39–41
indemnity, professional
  need and importance of
    insurance for, 60–61
institutions
  strengths and weaknesses of
    working in, 17–18
  see also particular e.g. National
    Health Service
instructions, therapy location
  importance of clarity and supply
    of, 5–7
insurance, business
  need for and importance,
    60–61
interest, therapist
  danger and consequences of, 86
  see also factors encouraging e.g.
    gifts; invitations, client
interruptions, doorbell
  need to make decisions
    concerning, 7–9
invitations, client
  danger and consequences of
    accepting, 87–8
  see also gifts
invoices and invoicing, client
  procedure and recording of,
    43–5

leaflets
  salience as marketing tool, 29

letters
  need for professionalism in
    writing of, 56–7
  need for thoughtful and
    considered responses, 81–2
  requirement and specifications of
    paper for, 55
locations, therapy
  features, strengths, and
    weaknesses of institutional,
    17–18
  features, strengths, and
    weaknesses of shared, 16–17
  possibilities for extending,
    80–81
  see also directions, therapy
    location
  see also specific locations and
    mediums e.g. home, therapist;
    National Health Service;
    telephone calls; therapy
    rooms

marketing
  methods of, 29–30
  role of personal reputation, 27–9
  see also specific tools e.g. registers,
    professional; websites; Yellow
    Pages
meetings, professional
  importance for refreshment and
    self development, 93–4
  salience and importance of
    attending, 114–15
meetings, therapy
  appropriate engagement at
    initial, 33–4
  tactfulness and sensitivity of
    initial, 34–6
  see also requirements e.g.
    boundaries, therapist-client;
    commitment, client

mistakes, therapist
  importance of avoiding, 115–16
money, client fees see fees, client

National Health Service
  strengths, and weaknesses of
    working within, 17–18
neatness
  importance of therapist personal
    appearance, 16
  requirement for paperwork and
    storage, 56
neighbours
  importance of protecting client
    privacy from, 72–3
non-payment, fee
  process of handling, 47–8
nosiness, therapist
  danger and consequences of, 86
notes and note taking
  importance of thoroughness and
    accuracy, 57
numbers, client
  need for schedule flexibility,
    106–7

openness, therapist-client
  need for in sessions only, 73–6

paper, letter writing
  requirement for and
    specifications, 55
paper trails
  importance of regular audit of,
    67–8
paperwork, business
  types and requirements for
    stationery, 54–5
  see also storage, paperwork
  see also factors required e.g.
    accuracy; confidentiality,
    client; neatness;

professionalism; reference,
  systems of
  see also particular paperwork e.g.
    audits, paper trail; letters;
    notes and note-taking
payments, fee
  methods and recording of,
    45–7
  need for policies for holiday
    period, 49–51
  need for policies on missed
    session, 51–3
  process of handling unpaid, 47–8
peacefulness
  importance in relation to therapy
    room, 10–11
  see also of factors affecting e.g.
    doorbells, interruptions by
peers
  role as source for comfort and
    refreshment, 95–6
practitioners, general
  role as source for comfort and
    advice, 94–5
privacy, client
  considerations in relation to
    waiting rooms, 12–13
  need to respect beyond sessions,
    70–73
professionalism
  importance in letters and note-
    taking, 56–9
  salience when expressing
    empathy and detachment,
    89–90
profile and reputation, personal
  methods of raising, 29–30
  salience as marketing tool,
    27–9
promotion, self-
  danger and consequences of,
    86–7

protection, third-party
  need and importance of
    insurance for, 60–61

quietness
  importance in relation to therapy
    room, 10–11
  see also of factors affecting e.g.
    doorbells, interruptions by

records and recording
  fee payments, 45–7
  see also particular records e.g. bills
    and billing, client
recuperation
  importance following illness,
    110–12
reference, systems of
  requirement for business
    paperwork, 56
refreshment, therapist
  importance of support systems
    enabling, 93–4
  see also sources e.g. events,
    external; families and friends;
    peers
refusal, session
  need for ability to engage in,
    118–19
registers, professional
  salience as marketing tool, 26–7,
    29
Relate (organisation), 24
reputation and profile, personal
  methods of raising, 29–30
  salience as marketing tool,
    27–9
restfulness
  importance in relation to therapy
    room, 10–11
  see also of factors affecting e.g.
    doorbells, interruptions by

retirement, therapist
  need to plan ahead before
    embarking on, 129–32
  options, advantages and
    disadvantages, 125–9, 132–4
review, client fees
  need for periodic, 42–3
rooms, consulting *see* therapy rooms

sabbaticals
  significance for practice survival,
    112
schedules, work
  need for flexibility of, 106–8
self-employment
  difficulties particular to
    therapists, 105–6
  salience of client number
    variability, 106–7
  need for client schedule
    flexibility, 107–10
  need for ability to refuse sessions,
    118–19
  salience of mistakes and
    enactments, 115–18
  see also factors affecting e.g.
    events, external; holidays
    and breaks; illness and
    incapacity
promotion, self-
  danger and consequences of,
    86–7
sensitivity, therapist
  need for at initial meeting, 34–6
sessions, therapy
  need for ability to refuse, 118–19
  need for policies on missed, 51–3
signposting, therapy room
  importance of supply and clarity
    of, 5–7
smartness, appearances of
  importance of therapist, 16

stationery
  nature of requirement for, 54–5
storage, paperwork
  requirement for neatness of, 56
  see also reference, systems of
supervision, therapist
  benefits of for practice and
    understanding, 92–3
support and comfort, therapist
  see comfort and support,
    therapist
surroundings, therapy *see* locations,
    therapy
systems, reference
  requirement for business
    paperwork, 56

tactfulness, therapist
  need for at initial meeting, 34–6
tax, income
  need and importance, 61–2
telephone calls
  handling of crisis calls, 83–4
  importance of clarity and
    boundary setting during, 82–3
  need for thoughtful and
    considered responses, 81–2
therapy and therapists
  importance of ensuring good first
    impressions, 13–14, 23–5
  importance of extraneous
    appropriate support, 98–100
  importance of maintaining
    health and well–being,
    100–104
  importance of smartness and
    neatness, 16
  narrative of process of, xvii–xx
  need for appropriate initial
    engagement, 31–6
  need to refrain from
    inappropriate support, 96–7

need to respect client privacy
beyond sessions, 70–73
role of GPs as source for comfort
and advice, 94–5
role of unconsciousness in
decision-making of, 112–13
salience of enactments for
practice, 116–18
special requirements of working
with couples, 84–5
see also boundaries, therapist-
client; endings, therapy;
refreshment, therapist;
retirement
tidiness and airiness
importance in relation to
therapy room, 11–12
time, therapist
see also elements e.g. businesses,
therapy; ethics; training,
therapist
see also factors affecting e.g.
age; illness and incapacity;
mistakes; refusal, session
therapy rooms
need for image of neutrality,
14–16
need for practical preparatory
decision-making, 2–4
possibilities for extending
location and space of, 80–81
see also specific considerations
e.g. access, therapy room;
cleanliness and airiness;
peacefulness
third parties
importance of insurance for
protection of, 60–61
thoughtfulness
importance in telephone,
email and letter contact,
81–2

time, therapist
need and importance of wisely
utilising, 68–9
need for boundary setting with
clients, 76–8
toilets
importance of appearance and
location, 10
training, therapist
importance in face of client
dissatisfaction, 90–91
role of theoretical underpinnings,
91
role and importance of therapy as
element of, 91
see also features e.g. supervision,
therapist
see also outcomes e.g. detachment;
empathy
see also specific e.g.
continuing professional
development
transfer, electronic
strengths and weaknesses as fee
payment method, 46–7

unconsciousness
role in therapy decision-making,
112–13

variability
salience as factor of self-
employment, 105–7

waiting rooms
considerations for client privacy
preservation, 12–13
websites
role as marketing tool, 30–31
well-being and health
need and importance of
maintenance of, 100–104

see also means e.g. exercise,
    therapist; holidays and breaks;
    refreshment, therapist
wills, professional
    need for and importance, 59–60

work and working *see* arrangements,
    working

Yellow Pages
    salience as marketing tool, 30

HYPNOTHERAPY
A Handbook
Second Edition

Michael Heap

9780335244454 (Paperback)
July 2012

eBook also available

"This is an excellent book. It is the best survey of the responsible practice of clinical hypnosis in the UK. The introduction, which provides an overview of theory and research about the nature of hypnosis, should be required reading for anyone practicing or training to practice in the field."
Irving Kirsch, Harvard Medical School, Beth Israel Deaconess Medical Center, USA, and University of Plymouth, UK

Key features:

- A new chapter on hypnotherapy and eating disorders
- An overview of theoretical understanding of hypnosis based on recent scientific evidence
- A variety of therapeutic techniques that may be tailored to individual clients

www.openup.co.uk

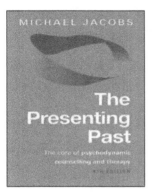

THE PRESENTING PAST
The Core of Psychodynamic
Counselling and Therapy
Fourth Edition

Michael Jacobs

9780335247189 (Paperback)
August 2012

eBook also available

In this new edition, Michael Jacobs gives psychodynamic counselling and therapy a truly human face. He brings practice to the forefront in a new three-part structure. This is realized through the swift introduction of the themes in the therapeutic relationship throughout the book, making integration of theory and practice clearer than ever. Looking at what the client presents as troubling them, what the therapist experiences about the client and their relationship in therapy and exploring theories to throw light on these themes now lies firmly at the core of the book.

Key features:

- A new structure takes the reader into the main themes more quickly and seeing them in practice in therapy.
- A series of sessions, beginning, middle and end, is introduced before the book proceeds to look at the way past experience influences presenting issues.
- Michel is committed to drawing on his lifetime's experience to enable psychodynamic counselling and therapy to have a truly human face.

www.openup.co.uk

OPEN UNIVERSITY PRESS
McGraw - Hill Education